ARE YOU READY FOR A
Miracle

JAMES MCFADDEN

A 21-DAY HEALING DEVOTIONAL

ARE YOU READY FOR A

Miracle

JAMES McFADDEN

A 21-DAY HEALING
DEVOTIONAL

BLAZE
PUBLISHING
MANSFIELD, TEXAS

ARE YOU READY FOR A MIRACLE?
A 21-Day Healing Devotional
by James A. McFadden

Published by Blaze Publishing House
www.blazepublishinghouse.com
BPH is a division of Ministry Solutions, LLC
P.O. Box 184
Mansfield, TX 76063
817.473.9704
www.msicreative.com

Unless otherwise noted, all Scripture quotations are taken from the King James Version of the Bible. Copyright © 1979, 1980, 1982 by Thomas Nelson, Inc., publishers. Used by permission.

Scripture quotations noted NKJV are taken from the New King James Version. Copyright © 1979, 1980, 1982, Thomas Nelson, Inc., Publishers.

Scripture quotations noted TLB are taken from The Living Bible. Copyright © 1971. Used by permission of Tyndale House Publishers, Inc., Wheaton, Illinois 60189.

Scripture quotations marked NLT are taken from the New Living Translation. Copyright © 1996. Used by permission of Tyndale House Publishers, Inc., Wheaton, Illinois 60189.

Scripture quotations marked NIV are taken from the Holy Bible, NEW INTERNATIONAL VERSION®. Copyright © 1973, 1978, 1984 International Bible Society. All rights reserved throughout the world. Used by permission of International Bible Society.

Library of Congress PCN: 2008932687

ISBN-13: 978-0-9792071-5-0
ISBN-10: 0-9792071-5-0

To a friend who was closer than a brother

John S. Underwood, II

He fought a good fight and kept the faith.

Acknowledgements

My most sincere appreciation to . . .

My wife, Brenda, for being my closest friend, most faithful supporter, wife, and mother of our children.

To our three children: Ashley, Thomas, and Marissa. You are each a special gift from God above. Thank you for sharing this call and making this a joyous journey.

To my parents, Pastor T. L. and Linda McFadden. Thank you for always practicing what you preached and living the Gospel each and every day. You both have poured an abundance of love and faith into my life.

To my apostle, Pastor Ron Morris. Thank you for the wealth of wisdom that you placed so freely at my disposal. Also, thank you for holding me accountable for the gift, the call, and legacy of the Holy Spirit.

To the executive board of Trinity Life Center. We are grateful beyond mere words. Your faithful trust and support has lifted us higher.

To the staff and membership of Trinity Life Center. Thank you for your unwavering and steadfast love. Brenda and I love each and every one of you.

To Pastor Mark Carter for your friendship and encouragement.

Thank you, Tammy Mercer and Cathy White, for your help with the manuscript.

Most of all, to the Lord Jesus Christ. Thank you for saving me. I love you more than words can say.

Table of Contents

Foreword   11

Introduction   13

DAY 1:   Does God Still Heal Today?   18

DAY 2:   Communion   26

DAY 3:   John G. Lake   35

DAY 4:   Why am I Sick?   42

DAY 5:   The Fear Factor   48

DAY 6:   Voices of Healing   59

DAY 7:   Spirits of Affliction   66

DAY 8:   Fervent Prayer   75

DAY 9:   Don't Confuse Your Faith
         with the Facts   81

DAY 10: Healing Forgiveness   90

DAY 11: Prescription Music   98

DAY 12: A Merry Heart 108

DAY 13: Smith Wigglesworth 114

DAY 14: The Windows of Heaven
         are Open 122

DAY 15: Help Thou My Unbelief 133

DAY 16: Take Action 142

DAY 17: Healing in the Old Testament 152

DAY 18: Divine Health. 159

DAY 19: Strong Defense. 168

DAY 20: The Key to Heaven 177

DAY 21: Hold On to Your Miracle! 184

Conclusion 191

Foreword

This devotional is a consolidation of Scriptural references to healing and a positive look into the promise made by a covenant God. Laced with testimony of past ministry and present faith, it is a powerful combination, placing the reader in touch with the mind of God on the issue of healing.

James McFadden is a friend. One of the highlights of my ministry is preaching in his church. We have traveled together into Jamaica and India. He is a man of God. The wisdom of his words far exceeds his age. His desire for the unveiled truth to find a home in your heart is evident in this book. By the time you complete the contents of this devotional, you will be inspired to believe and encouraged to stand. Your confidence will soar. Pastor James, like a shepherd, says, "Come, follow the Word of God."

The hope of this devotional is that it will prove helpful to all those desiring to have a fuller faith in God's power to heal. This book has an objective built into its topic: when you read this book, realize that a cloud of witnesses in the Bible would quickly say, "Amen!" Men like Isaiah, David, Peter, Paul, and Luke. Jesus, of course, is the Amen.

Apostle Ron Morris
Senior Pastor, Glad Tidings Church
Bangor, ME

Introduction

You are no doubt interested in experiencing God's miracle-working power in your life. Despite all the advances of modern medicine and the improvements made in easing the pain and suffering of the sick, there are still a vast number of people suffering today. Many Christians have resigned themselves to the fact they are just going to have to learn to live with their afflictions. I submit to you that you don't have to learn to live with it. Rather, you must learn that Christ died, so you can live without it!

So many today have been frustrated by the extreme limitations and exorbitant costs of healthcare. Often, the cure is worse than the malady. Many experience more discomfort and a myriad of symptoms brought on by the "cure." How frustrating is it to seek help from your physician, only to find his limited understanding of the human body that God created to be insufficient in bringing comfort and healing. I am grateful for the strides contemporary medical research has made; however, it often seems the more we delve into the human anatomy, the more we discover the mystery of God's wondrous, creative power.

According to Psalm 139:14, *"I will praise thee; for I am fearfully and wonderfully made: marvelous are thy works; and that my soul knoweth right well."*

This verse not only tells us what modern science continues to uncover—and it's very interesting they think they are the first to reveal it—but this verse also tells us something about what each of us knows deep down inside. *"My soul knoweth right well,"* confirms that each of us knows we were created by God. It is God alone who knows how to heal. After all, most of what we see in modern medicine is simply controlled trauma. They operate and remove something or insert something and then rely on the body's created immune system to heal and restore, hopefully better than when we started.

This devotional guide was designed to introduce you to the "Great Physician." My desire is to build your faith, line upon line and precept upon precept, and show you through study and example that our God is still in the healing business. Hopefully, you will come to see through the teachings of God's Word, as well as through insights from a few twentieth-century apostles, that our God has made provisions through the cross for your healing. I look forward to sharing my own personal testimony of our precious Savior's healing power. I will confront head-on the most common enemies of faith and offer hundreds of Scriptural references for meditation.

Regardless of whether you are battling cancer or a re-occurring headache, Christ holds the key to your miracle. This book is designed to read over a period of twenty-one days. Why twenty-one days? Because the number twenty-one has an important spiritual significance. Just look at the story of Daniel and his fast (Daniel 10:1-13).

Do you know why a Daniel fast lasts for twenty-one days? That number is taken from the amount of days Daniel fasted before he got the victory. Although God responded to Daniel's prayer the first day by sending a messenger, a powerful spiritual being of darkness detained the messenger for twenty-one days. Daniel faithfully continued praying and fasting, and God's messenger eventually arrived, assisted by the archangel, Michael.

Evil forces may challenge your prayers, but you must persist until there is a breakthrough. For Daniel, it took twenty-one days.

It's very interesting to note that most experts agree it takes twenty-one days to break an old habit and develop a new one. This is not a surprise to Bible scholars because the number "twenty-one" is the product of three times seven. "Three" is the number of God; He is the Holy Trinity. "Seven" is the number of completion and has also been called the number of rest, for God rested on the seventh day (Genesis 2:2). "Twenty-one" is, then, the number of divine completion—God's completed work in us. I like to think of "twenty-one" as the number of "breakthrough."

During my devotions one morning, the Lord began to impress very strongly upon me His tremendous desire to heal the sick. The movie, The *Passion of the Christ*, very powerfully illustrates the beating Christ endured for our healing. Isaiah 53:5 says, *"He was wounded for our transgressions . . . and by His stripes we are healed,"* (NKJV). The Holy Spirit helped me to picture in my mind a sea of hurting people on one side of a great chasm and Christ on the other side. Across this great divide was a bridge; on it was written a single word: faith. There was no real revelation in this image to a veteran preacher such as myself. I have preached that faith is a bridge, a ladder, a rope, and a life preserver and these are all good illustrations. But then, I noticed something very unique about the bridge. It had grown out of the side of the mountain and was very much a living tree.

This image sent my spirit racing. With all the talk about faith-building, although it is not wrong, we must be very careful not to stray too far from the very simple truth that faith is a Fruit of the Spirit.

Fruit cannot be manufactured in a laboratory; it must be cultivated. It may grow naturally of its own accord when given the right amount of nutrients and rain. The question I could not escape asking was: "Could faith, then, be cultivated in a greenhouse?" A greenhouse is a controlled environment which promotes growth. The temperature, moisture, soil density, and composition are all set to optimum levels. These factors do not guarantee growth, but they create an environment for success.

For the next twenty-one days, I would like to put your faith in a greenhouse, so to speak, sheltered from the world's harsh anti-faith environment. We are going to grow a "natural bridge" to the supernatural realm. The Lord's overwhelming desire to eliminate your suffering has already been demonstrated at Calvary. If you will allow the bridge of faith to grow across this great chasm of the carnal world, then you will be forever changed by the touch of the Master's hand.

Please forego the temptation to consume this in one sitting and follow the plan for daily meditation and devotional prayer. Some days may speak to you more than others; but somewhere along the way, you will find the key to your miracle. I am convinced if you will stay the course and continue daily in prayer and study, then at some point in your twenty-one days of consecration, the Lord will visit you.

"But unto you that fear my name shall the Sun of righteousness arise with healing in his wings; . . ."

Malachi 4:2

DAY 1

Does God Still Heal Today?

"... for I am the Lord that healeth thee."

Exodus 15:26

The answer is a resounding, "Yes, He does!" Healing is not only the will of God, it is His divine nature. Just as you have certain traits and idiosyncrasies that basically make you, you; one of the Lord's traits is His nature to heal. When something is part of your nature, you don't have to work at it or make yourself do it. It just flows out of you.

In the Old Testament, we see a tremendous amount of emphasis placed upon the name of an individual. In that name, we often see the character and nature of an individual revealed. Perhaps one of the best examples of this is found in Jacob whose name meant "supplanter," or what some might call a "flim-flam" man or charlatan. Sure enough, true to his name, Jacob bought his brother's birthright for a bowl of pottage and you've probably read the story of how that he tricked his father with lamb's wool. Esau must have been one hairy dude! What interests me is that when his character and nature changed, it coincided with a name change.

"And he said, Thy name shall be called no more Jacob, but Israel: for as a prince hast thou power with God and with men, and hast prevailed."

Genesis 32:28

God has revealed unto us His character and nature through His name, Jehovah Rapha—the Lord who heals, the healer, the physician.

". . . for I am the Lord that healeth thee."

Exodus 15:26

Some might assume that healings are unique to the New Testament. However, there are many instances of healing in the Old Testament, as well. Yes, the Lord did great miracles, such as the plagues of Egypt and the parting of the Red Sea in the book of Exodus. But, you might be surprised to read just how much is written about healing, too. When Israel left the land of Egypt and the bondage of slavery, the Bible says there was not a feeble one among them (Psalm 105:37). This is quite remarkable since we are talking about more than two million people.[1]

The Old Testament also tells us of a time when, through their rebellion and gluttony, the children of Israel began dying from snakebites. Gluttony is still a sure fire way to usher in sickness and suffering. The Lord told Moses to fashion a brass serpent upon a pole and the children of Israel would be healed when they looked at it.

"And the Lord said unto Moses, Make thee a fiery serpent, and set it upon a pole: and it shall come to pass, that every one that is

bitten, when he looketh upon it, shall live.
And Moses made a serpent of brass, and put
it upon a pole, and it came to pass, that if a
serpent had bitten any man, when he beheld
the serpent of brass, he lived."

Numbers 21:8-9

The serpent upon a cross remains to this day a
symbol of healing and medicine. We also know it was
a powerful symbol of Christ's victory on the cross.

"For he hath made him to be sin for us, who
knew no sin; that we might be made the
righteousness of God in him."

2 Corinthians 5:21

When a great baseball player or golfer has a fluid
swing that produces power, it's often referred to as a
"natural swing." Many describe Tiger Woods' swing
as "effortless." Well, the Lord is the home run
champion healer of all-time. Healing is effortless to
our God. It's more than just a part of His nature;
healing is His passion. The life of Jesus Christ gives
us an incredible glimpse into the heart of God. Jesus
said, *"I do the will of Him that sent Me,"* (John 4:34).

"But when he saw the multitudes, he was
moved with compassion on them, because
they fainted, and were scattered abroad, as
sheep having no shepherd."

Matthew 9:36

This reveals the will of Him who sent Christ. *". . .*
Jesus . . . went about doing good and healing all who
were sick and oppressed by the devil . . . ," (Acts

10:38). Christ said if you have seen Him, you have seen the Father (John 14:9).

Once we become certain beyond all doubt it is the Lord's nature to heal, then we have already answered the question: "Does God still heal today?" The Lord never changes. He is the same yesterday, today, and forever (Hebrews 13:8). Malachi 3:6, says, *"I change not."* A healing God who never changes is bound to do it again. You see, with God: once a healer, always a healer.

A healing God who never changes is bound to do it again.

Scripture Meditations

"Bless the Lord, O my soul: and all that is within me, bless his holy name. Bless the Lord, O my soul, and forget not all his benefits: Who forgiveth all thine iniquities; who healeth all thy diseases; Who redeemeth thy life from destruction; who crowneth thee with lovingkindness and tender mercies; Who satisfieth thy mouth with good things; so that thy youth is renewed like the eagle's."

Psalm 103:1-5

"Because thou hast made the Lord, which is my refuge, even the most High, thy habitation; There shall no evil befall thee, neither shall any plague come nigh thy dwelling. For he shall give his angels charge over thee, to keep thee in all thy ways."

Psalm 91:9-11

"And when Elisha was come into the house, behold, the child was dead, and laid upon his bed. He went in therefore, and shut the door upon them twain, and prayed unto the Lord. And he went up, and lay upon the child, and put his mouth upon his mouth, and his eyes upon his eyes, and his hands upon his hands: and he stretched himself upon the child; and the flesh of

the child waxed warm. Then he returned, and walked in the house to and fro; and went up, and stretched himself upon him: and the child sneezed seven times, and the child opened his eyes."

2 Kings 4:32-35

"So Naaman came with his horses and with his chariot, and stood at the door of the house of Elisha. And Elisha sent a messenger unto him, saying, Go and wash in Jordan seven times, and thy flesh shall come again to thee, and thou shalt be clean. But Naaman was wroth, and went away, and said, Behold, I thought, He will surely come out to me, and stand, and call on the name of the Lord his God, and strike his hand over the place, and recover the leper. Are not Abana and Pharpar, rivers of Damascus, better than all the waters of Israel? may I not wash in them, and be clean? So he turned and went away in a rage. And his servants came near, and spake unto him, and said, My father, if the prophet had bid thee do some great thing, wouldest thou not have done it? how much rather then, when he saith to thee, Wash, and be clean? Then went he down, and dipped himself seven times in Jordan, according to the saying of the man of God: and his flesh came again like unto the flesh of a little child, and he was clean."

2 Kings 5:9-14

"In those days was Hezekiah sick unto death. And Isaiah the prophet the son of Amoz came unto him, and said unto him, Thus saith the Lord, Set

thine house in order: for thou shalt die, and not live. Then Hezekiah turned his face toward the wall, and prayed unto the Lord, And said, Remember now, O Lord, I beseech thee, how I have walked before thee in truth and with a perfect heart, and have done that which is good in thy sight. And Hezekiah wept sore. Then came the word of the Lord to Isaiah, saying, Go, and say to Hezekiah, Thus saith the Lord, the God of David thy father, I have heard thy prayer, I have seen thy tears: behold, I will add unto thy days fifteen years."

Isaiah 38:1-5

"He brought them forth also with silver and gold: and there was not one feeble person among their tribes."

Psalm 105:37

"Who hath believed our report? and to whom is the arm of the Lord revealed? For he shall grow up before him as a tender plant, and as a root out of a dry ground: he hath no form nor comeliness; and when we shall see him, there is no beauty that we should desire him. He is despised and rejected of men; a man of sorrows, and acquainted with grief: and we hid as it were our faces from him; he was despised, and we esteemed him not. Surely he hath borne our griefs, and carried our sorrows: yet we did esteem him stricken, smitten of God, and afflicted. But he was wounded for our transgressions, he was bruised for our iniquities:

the chastisement of our peace was upon him; and with his stripes we are healed."

Isaiah 53:1-5

"As said, If thou wilt diligently hearken to the voice of the Lord thy God, and wilt do that which is right in his sight, and wilt give ear to his commandments, and keep all his statutes, I will put none of these diseases upon thee, which I have brought upon the Egyptians: for I am the Lord that healeth thee."

Exodus 15:26

DAY 2

Communion

"This do in remembrance of me."

1 Corinthians 11:24

The revelation of communion and how it relates to healing is critically important. You will be able to take full advantage of this teaching over the next few weeks, as well as for the rest of your life. This will begin a very extraordinary journey toward an ever-increasing faith in Christ's atonement.

There are two major components of the atonement—the blood and the body. Most Christians understand the power of the cross to atone for sin. Anyone who calls themselves a Christian must believe the cross brings victory over sin. Unfortunately, that is where their belief begins and ends. There is emotional and spiritual healing in the cross, but there is also physical healing in the atonement. Evidenced throughout Biblical history, as well as by modern-day testimonies, the blood was for salvation and the body was for healing. Healing in the atonement is discussed in several of the devotions in the next few weeks.

Today, let us turn our attention toward the study of daily communion. This simple, intimate act of remembrance could hold the key to unlocking your miracle. The thought of daily communion can seem strange if you have grown up in a typical, Protestant denomination. Even Charismatic and Pentecostal groups often under-emphasize the importance of Holy Communion. Many of these groups only administer the sacrament on holidays or once a month. Many times, their concern is the frequency; that if communion is served too often, it will somehow become mundane and commonplace. This concern is misguided. There is a direct connection between communion and healing. This Biblical revelation will set you on a course of divine health.

Let's begin with the Apostle Paul in 1 Corinthians 11:29-30: *"For he that eateth and drinketh unworthily, eateth and drinketh damnation to himself, not discerning the Lord's body. For this cause many are weak and sickly among you, and many sleep."*

Much sickness, and even death, in the early Church was because they were, *"not discerning the Lord's body."* The Corinthian church had already spiraled away from what the Lord's Supper was intended to be. It was not meant to ever be a gluttonous feast that discriminated against

. . . the blood was for salvation and the body was for healing.

fellow members. Much like today, communion had lost its humility and intimacy.

Remember, the Lord instituted this ordinance at the Passover. So much is inferred through the tremendous typology and history of the Jewish Feast of Passover that entire books have been written on the subject. Allow me to point out two very simple facts about the Passover meal: it was celebrated in the home and it was a family meal. This does not fit our modern-day model of communion one Sunday a month and that it must be administered through an ordained pastor or priest. Christ's last supper with His family and friends was a very intimate setting in which the bread and cup were passed around the table. I doubt they all did the "Da Vinci" pose on one side of the table, but rather sat with half on one side facing the other. Each one was no doubt accessible to Jesus as He offered His dish for dipping to the one who would betray Him.

The next thing to consider is the frequency of communion in the early Church.

"And they continued steadfastly in the apostles' doctrine and fellowship, and in breaking of bread, and in prayers."

Acts 2:42

This is in reference to the "apostles' doctrine" of breaking bread, not in reference to beating the Baptists to Burger King® after a church service. I can't tell you how many times I've heard Christians say they are going to go "break bread" and they are really on their way to Shoney's® after church.

"And they, continuing daily with one accord in the temple, and breaking bread from house to house, . . ."

Acts 2:46a

Here in verse forty-six, it is referenced again. This time it answers the question of frequency when it says, "daily." Daily communion from "house to house" (meaning in the home), was an integral part of worship in the early Church.

Jesus spoke of this when He taught His disciples how to pray. He said, *"Give us this day our daily bread,"* (Matthew 6:11). More than once Christ tells us He is the Bread of Life.[1]

> **"Then Jesus said unto them, Verily, verily, I say unto you, Except ye eat the flesh of the Son of man, and drink his blood, ye have no life in you. Whoso eateth my flesh, and drinketh my blood, hath eternal life; and I will raise him up at the last day. For my flesh is meat indeed, and my blood is drink indeed. He that eateth my flesh, and drinketh my blood, dwelleth in me, and I in him. As the living Father hath sent me, and I live by the Father: so he that eateth me, even he shall live by me. This is that bread which came down from heaven: not as your fathers did eat manna, and are dead: he that eateth of this bread shall live for ever."**
>
> **John 6:53-58**

Now, the children of Israel were instructed to gather just enough manna for one day, except on the day before the Sabbath. An angel fed the prophet a meal which gave him strength for forty days. The Lord could have given the children of Israel the same type of meal, but He chose the daily manna. Manna was a type of pattern God used to indicate the need for daily communion and fellowship with Him.

I'm not trying to teach a new doctrine, but am only attempting to release people to enjoy the spiritual and healing benefits of daily communion. Many theologians agree that communion was a central part of all first-century gatherings. Congregational communion was not meant to replace communion in the home. This is where we have erred. Jesus did say, *". . . As often as you do this, . . . ,"* in reference to communion (1 Corinthians 11:25). Religion has taught us that no one except an ordained pastor or priest may administer the sacraments. This conflicts with one very important verse in the Bible. 1 Peter 2:9 says, *"But ye are a chosen generation, a royal priesthood, an holy nation, a peculiar people; that ye should shew forth the praises of him who hath called you out of darkness into his marvellous light:"*

This verse makes clear the priesthood of every believer. Not to mention, it was the leader of each household who applied the blood on the doorposts at Passover, not a Levite. There is no place in the New Testament where the Church is instructed to restrict the administering of communion to ordained ministers.

Who among us would not have faith to receive a miracle if we could physically touch Jesus like the woman with the issue of blood? Communion bread has given us a way to touch Christ's body, not through transubstantiation, but through transignification, faith, and remembrance.[2] To discern the Lord's body means more than the protocol by which we receive communion. This also speaks to our faith and spiritual emphasis as we receive communion. We might be healed when we clearly understand the amazing amount of suffering Christ endured. When that understanding comes, then we will not allow His back to be beaten in vain.

Be encouraged to gather the simple elements of the Lord's Supper, some unleavened bread or crackers and some fruit of the vine (red grape juice.) Draw together your family and share communion right now in your home. Remember to ask the Lord for His forgiveness and cleansing so you don't take it unworthily. Bless the bread and wine. Allow the promises of salvation and healing in the atonement to be refreshed in your heart as you partake. Take communion every day during your devotion time for the rest of this twenty-one day devotional guide.

Scripture Meditations

"Then came the day of unleavened bread, when the passover must be killed. And he sent Peter and John, saying, Go and prepare us the passover, that we may eat. And they said unto him, Where wilt thou that we prepare? And he said unto them, Behold, when ye are entered into the city, there shall a man meet you, bearing a pitcher of water; follow him into the house where he entereth in. And ye shall say unto the goodman of the house, The Master saith unto thee, Where is the guestchamber, where I shall eat the passover with my disciples? And he shall shew you a large upper room furnished: there make ready. And they went, and found as he had said unto them: and they made ready the passover. And when the hour was come, he sat down, and the twelve apostles with him. And he said unto them, With desire I have desired to eat this passover with you before I suffer: For I say unto you, I will not any more eat thereof, until it be fulfilled in the kingdom of God. And he took the cup, and gave thanks, and said, Take this, and divide it among yourselves: For I say unto you, I will not drink of the fruit of the vine, until the kingdom of God shall come. And he took bread, and gave thanks, and brake it, and gave unto them, saying, This is my body which is given for you: this do in remembrance of me. Likewise also the cup after supper, saying, This cup is the new testament in my blood, which is shed for you."

Luke 22:7-20

"And they shall take of the blood, and strike it on the two side posts and on the upper door post of the houses, wherein they shall eat it. And they shall eat the flesh in that night, roast with fire, and unleavened bread; and with bitter herbs they shall eat it. Eat not of it raw, nor sodden at all with water, but roast with fire; his head with his legs, and with the purtenance thereof. And ye shall let nothing of it remain until the morning; and that which remaineth of it until the morning ye shall burn with fire. And thus shall ye eat it; with your loins girded, your shoes on your feet, and your staff in your hand; and ye shall eat it in haste: it is the LORD'S passover."

Exodus 12:7-11

"Who his own self bore our sins in his own body on the tree, that we, being dead to sins, should live unto righteousness: by whose stripes ye were healed."

1 Peter 2:24

"And when he had given thanks, he brake it, and said, Take, eat: this is my body, which is broken for you: this do in remembrance of me. After the same manner also he took the cup, when he had supped, saying, This cup is the new testament in my blood: this do ye, as oft as ye drink it, in remembrance of me. For as often as ye eat this bread, and drink this cup, ye do shew the Lord's death till he come. Wherefore whosoever shall eat this bread, and drink this cup of the Lord, unworthily, shall be guilty of the body and blood of the Lord. But let a man examine himself, and so

let him eat of that bread, and drink of that cup. For he that eateth and drinketh unworthily, eateth and drinketh damnation to himself, not discerning the Lord's body. For this cause many are weak and sickly among you, and many sleep."

1 Corinthians 11:24-30

John G. Lake

"When the even was come, they brought unto
him many that were possessed with devils:
and he cast out the spirits with his word, and
healed all that were sick:"

Matthew 8:16

John G. Lake, one of this past century's greatest
apostles of healing, was quoted as saying, "When
I saw for the first time by the Word of God that
sickness was not the will of God . . . everything in my
nature rose up to defeat the will of the devil."[1] Wow!
What a powerful statement. In 1898, under the
ministry of Alexander Dowie, John G. Lake witnessed
the instantaneous healing of his wife from tubercu-
losis. This was not the first healing Lake had
witnessed, but it proved to be a turning point in his
life. Nine years later, Lake received the baptism in
the Holy Spirit. He felt God directing him to Africa
where he ministered from 1908 to 1913.

Fortunately for us, Lake kept a journal through
much of his ministry. It is filled with incredible first-
hand accounts of the miracle-working power of God.
One entry reads:

"Sunday, November 27, 1910.

"A young man who had been ill from sun-stroke was brought to the tabernacle from Potchefstroom. He had suffered for six months with violent pains in his head. The dear Lord healed him as Vanderwall, Heroldt and I prayed and laid hands on him."[2]

Another journal entry dated Wednesday, November 30, 1910 says:

"At the tabernacle meeting a widow lady, Mrs. Bosman, came in great distress, knelt at the altar, and cried, 'My baby (about 2 and a half to 3 years old) is dying. Won't you pray? Won't you pray? We all went to prayer. The demon powers were very active. A mighty wave of rebuke in the Spirit came on me. The baby was at Mrs. Freslich's home, 30 Silian Road, Fiordsburg. The doctor said it was poisoned, having eaten something. I felt it' and as we arose I said to her, Go on home, dear Sister. Look up; your baby is all right.' She begged me to come in the morning, and I did. I found that as we prayed at the tabernacle the night before, the child had fallen sound asleep, was healed, and was now well and walking about. Mrs. Bosman, Mrs. Freslich, and I knelt and gave thanks to God for His goodness."[3]

Lake launched what has been documented as the "most extensive and powerful missionary movement in all of Africa!"[4] He returned to the United States having suffered the loss of his beloved wife and began a work in Spokane, Washington. It is estimated that thousands of healings occurred through Lake's ministry during the next five or six years.

Lake captured the heart of Christ when he called sickness "the will of the devil." After all, the Word of God declared in 1 John 3:8, *". . . for this purpose the Son of God was manifested, that he might destroy the works of the devil." "How God anointed Jesus of Nazareth with the Holy Ghost and with power: who went about doing good, and healing all that were oppressed of the devil; . . . ,"* (Acts 10:38).

No wonder Lake's ministry was effective in healing the sick. He considered sickness, in any form, to be an affront to God's will. It's easy to pray with confidence when you know you are praying the perfect will of God. All efforts to convince God

Every moment of sickness and pain is thievery.

are abandoned and our faith is concentrated on defeating the will of the anti-christ. The shield of faith is effective and provides the optimum protection when it faces the enemy.

We see through the Word that there are two diametrically opposed plans for your life.

"The thief cometh not, but for to steal, and to kill, and to destroy: I am come that they might have life, and that they might have it more abundantly."

John 10:10

Every moment of sickness and pain is thievery. Your rights as a covenant believer are being violated. Lake took a position of warfare, *". . . a mighty wave of rebuke in the spirit came on me. . . . We prayed; my spirit seemed to grapple with the devil. He was overthrown."*[5] Are you prepared to fight the demons of affliction and fear for your healing? Will you "take by force" the promise of your miracle, according to Matthew 11:12?

> **"Ye are of God, little children, and have overcome them: because greater is he that is in you, than he that is in the world."**

> **1 John 4:4**

May the Spirit of Christ arise within you in a righteous rage to oppose Satan's evil onslaught. Let every fiber of your being stand against the enemy of your soul and body. Admonish every thought as if it were an evil spirit that allows any concession to God's perfect will for your body. Accept nothing less than Lucifer's unconditional surrender. I call forth from your spirit an anointed rebuke which will rattle hell's gates; confounding the enemy and allowing the blessings of God to flow into your life unobstructed.

Scripture Meditations

"How God anointed Jesus of Nazareth with the Holy Ghost and with power: who went about doing good, and healing all that were oppressed of the devil; for God was with him."

Acts 10:38

"And from the days of John the Baptist until now the kingdom of heaven suffereth violence, and the violent take it by force."

Matthew 11:12

"Behold! I have given you authority and power to trample upon serpents and scorpions, and [physical and mental strength and ability] over all the power that the enemy [possesses]; and nothing shall in any way harm you."

Luke 10:19 (AMP)

"Submit yourselves therefore to God. Resist the devil, and he will flee from you."

James 4:7

"And hath raised us up together, and made us sit together in heavenly places in Christ Jesus:"

Ephesians 2:6

"And so it is written, The first man Adam was made a living soul; the last Adam was made a quickening spirit. Howbeit that was not first which is spiritual, but that which is natural; and afterward that which is spiritual. The first man is of the earth, earthy: the second man is the Lord from heaven."

1 Corinthians 15:45-47

"And when Jesus was entered into Capernaum, there came unto him a centurion, beseeching him, And saying, Lord, my servant lieth at home sick of the palsy, grievously tormented. And Jesus saith unto him, I will come and heal him. The centurion answered and said, Lord, I am not worthy that thou shouldest come under my roof: but speak the word only, and my servant shall be healed. For I am a man under authority, having soldiers under me: and I say to this man, Go, and he goeth; and to another, Come, and he cometh; and to my servant, Do this, and he doeth it. When Jesus heard it, he marvelled, and said to them that followed, Verily I say unto you, I have not found so great faith, no, not in Israel. And I say unto you, That many shall come from the east and west, and shall sit down with Abraham, and Isaac, and Jacob, in the kingdom of heaven. But the children of the kingdom shall be cast out into outer darkness: there shall be weeping and gnashing of teeth. And Jesus said unto the centurion, Go thy

way; and as thou hast believed, so be it done unto thee. And his servant was healed in the selfsame hour."

Matthew 8:5-13

DAY 4

Why am I Sick?

"Beloved, if our heart condemn us not, then
have we confidence toward God."

1 John 3:21

Why am I sick? This is a question far too many Christians are asking themselves. "Why" is an accusation of sorts. "Why" is to question the motive of an individual. It can be an indictment of self. Satan is the accuser of the brethren and we can find ourselves assisting in his mission to tear down our faith and confidence towards God.

Faith towards God and condemnation towards self do not flow together. You must come to terms with the truth that you are not sick because you are being punished or there are hidden sins in your life.

Christ's disciples were just as confused as many of today's Christians about this issue of "why."

"And as Jesus passed by, he saw a man which was blind from his birth. And his disciples asked him, saying, Master, who did sin, this man, or his parents, that he was born blind? Jesus answered, neither hath this man sinned, nor his parents: but that the works of

God should be made manifest in him. I must work the works of him that sent me, while it is day: the night cometh, when no man can work. As long as I am in the world, I am the light of the world. When he had thus spoken, he spat on the ground, and made clay of the spittle, and he anointed the eyes of the blind man with the clay."

John 9:1-6

The disciples got caught up in playing the blame game. We, as humans, seem obsessed with: "Who done it?" When are we going to realize that sickness is not God's whip; it is Satan's arrow? Isaiah 58:8-9, *"Then shall thy light break forth as the morning, and thine health shall spring forth speedily: . . . Then shalt thou call, and the Lord shall answer; thou shalt cry, and he shall say, Here I am. If thou take away from the midst of thee the yoke, the putting forth of the finger . . ."* If we are going to experience divine health, we must stop looking for something or someone to point our finger towards.

> When are we going to realize that sickness is not God's whip; it is Satan's arrow?

Without absolute confidence in the atoning power of Christ's blood, our suspicious mind will search tirelessly for even the hint of impropriety, banging the gavel down in judgment of our lack of self-control. "How might God, in all fairness, heal someone who doesn't pray enough or fast enough or who doesn't eat right?" Our lists of charges are too many to name, but the sentence is clear—no healing for us. One simple, but powerful, truth stands in stark opposition to this mental courtroom drama.

"God forbid: yea, let God be true, but every man a liar; as it is written, That thou mightest be justified in thy sayings, and mightest overcome when thou art judged."

Romans 3:4

Acts 13:39 tells us, *"And by him all that believe are justified from all things, from which ye could not be justified by the law of Moses."* The meaning of the word "justified" is "just as if I never sinned." Is it possible that many of us have confused justification with sanctification? The blessings of God are not based upon your sanctification. Strong's Exhaustive Concordance gives us the following definition of the New Testament Greek word "sanctify" or "agiazw" (hagiazo, hag-ee-ad'-zo), which means: *to render or acknowledge, or to be venerable or hallow.*[1] *The New Webster's Expanded Dictionary* defines "render": *to give in return; to give back; to present; to afford; to invest with qualities; to translate; to interpret; to clarify, as tallow.*[2]

Sanctification is the process of setting ourselves apart for the Lord's service in return or response to the amazing grace that has justified us completely. Some have misled others into thinking that salvation is more of a process of conversion, that one grows into salvation and only after time they receive the full benefits of that salvation.

If you are suffering today and you are a believer, righteousness is not the issue. It is far more likely that the issue is more a matter of confidence toward God's promise than some unsanctified area of your life. The grace of God has made you just. Webster defines just as right, acting rightly, upright one might say righteous.[3] Do you struggle to see yourself as righteous as Jesus Christ? Study these few verses and ponder the righteousness of Christ in you. Whenever you pray, do so in complete confidence of your right to access your inheritance. He whom the Son sets free is free indeed.[4] The righteous have a right to healing. I can't help but think of the worship chorus that says:

"You are all my righteousness
I stand complete in you and worship you.
You are all my righteousness
I stand complete in you, and worship you.
You are all my righteousness
I stand complete in you
and worship Christ my King.
Worship Him, Christ the Lord."[5]

Stop trying to purchase your miracle with your good works. Nothing you could ever do would make you worthy of His touch. Become completely dependent on Christ's righteousness and enter the presence of your Heavenly Father knowing He will grant your request based on Christ's obedience at Calvary.

Scripture Meditations

"Even the righteousness of God which is by faith of Jesus Christ unto all and upon all them that believe: for there is no difference:"

Romans 3:22

"For if by one man's offence death reigned by one; much more they which receive abundance of grace and of the gift of righteousness shall reign in life by one, Jesus Christ.)"

Romans 5:17

"For they being ignorant of God's righteousness, and going about to establish their own righteousness, have not submitted themselves unto the righteousness of God."

Romans 10:3

"For with the heart man believeth unto righteousness; and with the mouth confession is made unto salvation."

Romans 10:10

"For he hath made him to be sin for us, who knew no sin; that we might be made the righteousness of God in him."

2 Corinthians 5:21

"I do not frustrate the grace of God: for if righteousness come by the law, then Christ is dead in vain."

Galatians 2:21

"And be found in him, not having mine own righteousness, which is of the law, but that which is through the faith of Christ, the righteousness which is of God by faith:"

Philippians 3:9

"Not by works of righteousness which we have done, but according to his mercy he saved us, by the washing of regeneration, and renewing of the Holy Ghost;"

Titus 3:5

Day 5

The Fear Factor

"Say to them that are of a fearful heart, Be strong, fear not:
behold, your God will come with vengeance, even God with a
recompence; he will come and save you."

Isaiah 35:4

F ear is anti-faith. Fear will, without question, impact your ability to receive from the Lord. Great attention must be given to identifying the areas of your heart which may be subject to fear. God has not given us the spirit of fear (2 Timothy 1:7). There are two specific things revealed in this verse of Scripture:

1. Fear is a spirit, and

2. God is NOT the origin of fear.

These two simple facts have long-lasting implications if we are to understand how to battle fear effectively.

The Bible says fear will torment us (1 John 4:18). This is true on many levels. Things don't torment us; fear itself does. Fear paralyzes and preoccupies. Because of fear, our imagination focuses on the worst possible outcome. It sucks our faith out of us just like a nail does in a brand new tire. Until we aggressively declare war on the spirit of fear, it will rape and plunder our miracle promises.

Exposing fear and anxiety to the truth of God's Word is your most powerful offensive weapon. Fear often cloaks itself in the fashion of "wise counsel" and "common sense." Although wisdom is a prize to be sought after, true wisdom is heavenly not earthly. Sometimes what we teach as "wisdom" is really doubt in disguise.

> **"Beloved, believe not every spirit, but try the spirits whether they are of God: . . ."**
>
> **1 John 4:1**

Remember, fear is a spirit and God is NOT the origin of fear. The wisdom of God will not cause you to be moved by fear but will require you to walk by faith.

> **"But without faith it is impossible to please him: for he that cometh to God must believe that he is, and that he is a rewarder of them that diligently seek him."**
>
> **Hebrews 11:6**

Fear often cloaks itself in the fashion of "wise counsel" and "common sense."

I find it a bit ironic that President Teddy Roosevelt, who shares his first name with the cuddly crib protector, the Teddy Bear, made famous the African proverb, "Speak softly and carry a big stick."

> **"And take the helmet of salvation, and the sword of the Spirit, which is the word of God:"**

> **Ephesians 6:17**

As a believer, we have the right to carry the Word of almighty God. The Word is our spiritual sword; a spiritual, concealed, deadly weapon. We are less likely to walk in fear when we are trained and skilled in how to use the Word of God effectively. We can head off fear at the pass with the Word of God. Fear is like every other spirit: if you feed it, it will grow. Fear can literally become a monster, of sorts, if given the right nutrition.

What do you think a fear monster would eat? Perhaps nothing but soy burgers and raw vegetables—after all, everything else causes cancer and death, right? That is kind of how fear works. It gathers just enough information for you to fixate on the potential danger until mere possibilities become, in your mind, absolute certainties. Did you know there are hundreds of words which categorize the various psychological disorders associated with fear? Some examples are apeirophobia: fear of infinity; arachibutyrophobia: fear of peanut butter sticking to the roof of the mouth; or, even politicophobia: fear of politicians, which I can kind of understand a healthy fear of politicians; those guys are scary.[1]

Perhaps the one most germane to our discussion is the person who is always afraid of being sick, the hypochondriac. Unrealistic fear of illness can be paralyzing and it is certainly nothing to joke about. Most of you would never be diagnosed a hypochondriac; but yet, if you truly believe the Word of God, any fear of sickness is not warranted for a believer. The Word declares in Psalms 91:10, *"There shall no evil befall thee, neither shall any plague come nigh thy dwelling."*

National Statistics on Stress[2]

✓   Stress accounts for over $30 billion in medical and disability payments and over $99 billion in productivity loss.

✓   Stress keeps about one million people a day from going to work.

✓   Stress causes 1/3 of American workers to seriously consider quitting their jobs.

✓   75% of reported high-frequency illness in employees is stress-related.

✓   85% of employee accidents are stress-related.

A battle line must be drawn on the map of our mind. We must confront every thought that even hints of fear.

There are very strong spiritual overtones to the amazing statistics which show that stress, worry, and anxiety are major contributors to declining health. High blood pressure, heart disease, ulcers, intestinal disorders, shingles, cold sores, migraines, and a host of others illnesses are either brought on or increased by stress and fear. We must develop a Biblical plan of attack against the onslaught of fear.

"There is no fear in love; but perfect love casteth out fear: because fear hath torment. He that feareth is not made perfect in love."

1 John 4:18

Therefore, if fear is the problem, then love is the answer. It is a beautiful thing to see the absolute trust and confidence a child places in its parents. Babies seem to know mom or dad is going to catch them when they fall. This can make them seem fearless. As a parent of three, let me tell you something. You better be a watchin'. Our babies would simply free-fall off the couch with every confidence that ole' dad would catch them. They seemed fearless. The pure and untainted love of a child gives them tremendous power over even the natural fear of falling. This is an example of how each of us could potentially trust our Heavenly Father with even our natural fears of illness or even death.

"For ye have not received the spirit of bondage again to fear; but ye have received

the Spirit of adoption, whereby we cry, Abba, Father."

Romans 8:15

Perfect love may seem mysterious to some. After all, what love is without its reservations and question marks? But that child's love is not measured against a lifetime of frustrations and disappointments. Often, it is the hurts of family, friends, and lovers that create barriers of distrust and suspicion. We must realize that man is fallible, but God is infallible. Man is inconsistent, but God is the same yesterday, today, and forever (Hebrews 13:8).

Man is prone to lie but God is neither a man that He should lie nor the Son of Man that He should repent (Numbers 23:19). If you leap off the comfortable couch of convalescence, Abba Father (Daddy) will catch you! Measure your fear factor in the light of these few verses:

Scripture Meditations

"Ye shall not fear them: for the LORD your God he shall fight for you."

Deuteronomy 3:22

"Be strong and of a good courage, fear not, nor be afraid of them: for the LORD thy God, he it is that doth go with thee; he will not fail thee, nor forsake thee."

Deuteronomy 31:6

"Have not I commanded thee? Be strong and of a good courage; be not afraid, neither be thou dismayed: for the LORD thy God is with thee whithersoever thou goest."

Joshua 1:9

"And David said to Solomon his son, Be strong and of good courage, and do it: fear not, nor be dismayed: for the LORD God, even my God, will be with thee; he will not fail thee, nor forsake thee, until thou hast finished all the work for the service of the house of the LORD."

1 Chronicles 28:20

"And he said, Hearken ye, all Judah, and ye inhabitants of Jerusalem, and thou king Jehoshaphat, Thus saith the Lord unto you, Be not afraid nor dismayed by reason of this great multitude; for the battle is not yours, but God's."

2 Chronicles 20:15

"The LORD is my light and my salvation; whom shall I fear? the LORD is the strength of my life; of whom shall I be afraid?"

Psalm 27:1

" The LORD is on my side; I will not fear: what can man do unto me?"

Psalm 118:6

"Fear thou not; for I am with thee: be not dismayed; for I am thy God: I will strengthen thee; yea, I will help thee; yea, I will uphold thee with the right hand of my righteousness."

Isaiah 41:10

"In righteousness shalt thou be established: thou shalt be far from oppression; for thou shalt not fear: and from terror; for it shall not come near thee."

Isaiah 54:14

"But fear not thou, O my servant Jacob, and be not dismayed, O Israel: for, behold, I will save thee from afar off, and thy seed from the land of their captivity; and Jacob shall return, and be in rest and at ease, and none shall make him afraid."

Jeremiah 46:27

"Then said he unto me, Fear not, Daniel: for from the first day that thou didst set thine heart to understand, and to chasten thyself before thy God, thy words were heard, and I am come for thy words."

Daniel 10:12

"Fear not, O land; be glad and rejoice: for the LORD will do great things."

Joel 2:21

"Are not two sparrows sold for a farthing? and one of them shall not fall on the ground without your Father. But the very hairs of your head are all numbered. Fear ye not therefore, ye are of more value than many sparrows."

Matthew 10:29-31

"While he yet spake, there cometh one from the ruler of the synagogue's house, saying to him, Thy daughter is dead; trouble not the Master. But when Jesus heard it, he answered him, saying,

Fear not: believe only, and she shall be made whole."

Luke 8:49

"Fear not, little flock; for it is your Father's good pleasure to give you the kingdom."

Luke 12:32

"So that we may boldly say, The Lord is my helper, and I will not fear what man shall do unto me."

Hebrews 13:6

"There is no fear in love; but perfect love casteth out fear: because fear hath torment. He that feareth is not made perfect in love."

1 John 4:18

"Thou shalt not be afraid for the terror by night; nor for the arrow that flieth by day;"

Psalm 91:5

"He shall not be afraid of evil tidings: his heart is fixed, trusting in the LORD."

Psalm 112:7

"But straightway Jesus spake unto them, saying, Be of good cheer; it is I; be not afraid."

Matthew 14:27

"Peace I leave with you, my peace I give unto you: not as the world giveth, give I unto you. Let not your heart be troubled, neither let it be afraid."

John 14:27

Voices of Healing

"There is one who speaks like the piercings
of a sword, but the tongue of the wise
promotes health. . . . Anxiety in the heart of
man causes depression, but a good word
makes it glad."

Proverbs 12:18, 25 (NKJV)

There is a healing power in words. While watching a television special on medicine, I found it fascinating that studies have been done with placebos (sugar pills) to determine the importance of a doctor having a good bedside manner.[1] The participants of the study were given the same placebo but they were told something different from their doctor. One group was told they could try this "medicine" and it may or may not work. The other group was told this "medicine" would definitely work. The results showed the placebo was fifty percent more effective in the cases where they were given a positive word. The commentator jokingly said that if nothing else, it's important to get a positive doctor. This study does help illustrate the healing power of words.

It is so important that you surround yourself with people who support your faith, not your disease.

Job's friends came to comfort him and ended up making him feel worse, eventually bringing the judgment of God upon themselves for their negativism and accusations.

> *"My friends scorn me: but mine eye poureth out tears unto God."*
>
> **Job 16:20**

With friends like that, who needs enemies? I am certain they had the best intentions, but they continued to speak things Job knew in his heart weren't true. When you know the truth—that by His stripes you were healed—it doesn't help to have someone speaking negatively into your ear. Guard your heart from words of condemnation and accusation.

> It is so important that you surround yourself with people who support your faith, not your disease

More important than what you hear is what you say. The words of your mouth will bear fruit.

> *"I create the fruit of the lips; Peace, peace to him that is far off, and to him that is near, saith the LORD; and I will heal him."*
>
> **Isaiah 57:19**

You must begin each day with words of faith and affirmation that you are well in Jesus' name. Do not allow words of doubt and unbelief to come out of your mouth.

"Out of the same mouth proceedeth blessing and cursing. My brethren, these things ought not so to be."

James 3:10

Do you realize that you have the power to curse yourself?

"I don't think I'm going to make it."

"I don't know what is wrong with me"

"I can't take this any more."

"I'm sick and tired."

These phrases are just a few examples of the condemnation you can place on yourself.

Recently, when on vacation, a young man at my church called asking if I would bail him out of jail with five hundred dollars. He told us he was pulled over by the police for speeding and they suspended his license, and then locked him up. I told him we would work something out. He started to laugh and said he was just kidding. My wife and I did not think it was funny. We were fully prepared to leave our vacation early and go help this young man. After we returned from vacation, we invited him over to the house. He replied that he couldn't make it because he was working to repay a bill. He then explained that the night after he had pranked us on the phone, he was pulled over for doing thirty miles over the speed limit. He had a teenager in the car with him and was charged with wanton endangerment. They suspended his license and locked him up—and set the bail at five hundred dollars! I told him that was down-right scary. If you don't want it, then don't say it! Don't even joke about it!

While returning home to Louisville from Bangor, Maine, I was seated next to evangelist Dwight Jones, a famous harmonica player. We were discussing the great healing revivals of the past and he shared some wonderful testimonies about Reverend Jack Coe. Jones revealed that his father worked in the prayer tents during many of Reverend Coe's meetings. Although he was a young boy at the time, he could still remember many testimonies. I asked him, "Why don't we see the miracles and healing that we used to in the church?" His reply confirmed my desire and unction to write this devotional. Jones said that he had the opportunity to ask, now, the late Ruth Heflin that same question. She wrote several books on the glory, was part of the Brownsville Revival, and was—and still is—highly respected by Benny Hinn. Mother Heflin said, "I don't really know." Jones followed up by asking, "Do you think, Mother, that it could be because we don't prepare the hearts of the people the way that we used to?" She threw her head back and responded, "That is it! That is it, Brother Dwight. The Holy Spirit bears witness to that."

Jones' father spent many hours in the prayer tents of men like Jack Coe and A. A. Allen as they taught on healing. The sick and those who were there for a miracle would sit for hours before and after the services while every verse in the Bible on healing was read aloud. The Bible says in Hebrews 11:1, "Now faith comes by hearing and hearing by the Word of God." Your heart needs to be prepared with words of hope and faith in the power of God to heal the sick.

"The wicked is ensnared by the transgression of his lips, but the righteous will come through trouble. . . . He who speaks truth declares righteousness, but a false witness, deceit."

Proverbs 12:13, 17 (NKJV)

This also serves to illustrate the power of your words. Within your words are the living miracle seeds that will produce a harvest of healing. If care is given to watching your words, an atmosphere of faith and expectancy can be constructed that helps control the environment so miracle seeds can grow without fear of abortion. This greenhouse effect is a very important part of your miracle process. Don't underestimate the importance of what you say even in brief moments of emotional discouragement.

Make it a conscious effort to speak the Word of God over your situation every day. This is like the gentle morning rain of spring. It waters the seed and creates an atmosphere for growth. Weeds are sown through words of doubt and criticism. These weeds grow quickly and choke the life out of your promises. Everything you speak out of your mouth is a seed.

Are you sowing healing and life or discouragement and death? Are you a voice of healing for yourself and those around you? You will not only reap what you sow; you will reap what you say. Take a moment to study these few verses on the incredible impact of words:

Scripture Meditations

"For verily I say unto you, that whosoever shall say unto this mountain, Be thou removed, and be thou cast into the sea; and shall not doubt in his heart, but shall believe that those things which he saith shall come to pass; he shall have whatsoever he saith."

Mark 11:23

"And when Jesus was entered into Capernaum, there came unto him a centurion, beseeching him, And saying, Lord, my servant lieth at home sick of the palsy, grievously tormented. And Jesus saith unto him, I will come and heal him. The centurion answered and said, Lord, I am not worthy that thou shouldest come under my roof: but speak the word only, and my servant shall be healed. For I am a man under authority, having soldiers under me: and I say to this man, Go, and he goeth; and to another, Come, and he cometh; and to my servant, Do this, and he doeth it. When Jesus heard it, he marvelled, and said to them that followed, Verily I say unto you, I have not found so great faith, no, not in Israel. And I say unto you, That many shall come from the east and west, and shall sit down with Abraham, and Isaac, and Jacob, in the kingdom of heaven. But the children of the kingdom shall be cast out into outer darkness: there shall be weeping and gnashing of teeth. And Jesus said unto the centurion, Go thy

way; and as thou hast believed, so be it done unto thee. And his servant was healed in the selfsame hour."

Matthew 8:5-13

"He sent his word, and healed them, and delivered them from their destructions."

Psalm 107:20

"When the even was come, they brought unto him many that were possessed with devils: and he cast out the spirits with his word, and healed all that were sick:"

Matthew 8:16

"And they were astonished at his doctrine: for his word was with power."

Luke 4:32

Day 7
Spirits of Affliction

"How God anointed Jesus of Nazareth with the
Holy Ghost and with power: who went about doing good,
and healing all that were oppressed of the devil;
for God was with him."

Acts 10:38

The Bible plainly teaches there are spirits of affliction. In Mark, we read about a dumb and deaf spirit which Christ cast out of a young boy. This should not surprise most of us that the devil is in the business of afflicting humanity. After all, this seems to be the main objective of Satan since his fall.

"The thief cometh not, but for to steal, and to kill, and to destroy: I am come that they might have life, and that they might have it more abundantly."

John 10:10

Perhaps the real issue that many grapple with is whether evil spirits exists at all. And if they do, what are they? I'm not interested in tackling that subject in this setting, but I would like to make a few general comments about demons. The word "demon" is not found anywhere in the King James Version, but it is found in more modern translations. The King James Version does, however, mention devils, foul spirits, evil spirits, lying spirits, and others. The word "demon" according to Webster means *"a spirit, holding a place below the celestial deities of the pagans; an evil spirit; a devil; a fiend-like man."*[1] Many instances of demonic manifestations are mentioned in Scripture. Some were lunatics and some might conclude that first-century demons were only Man's attempt to explain insanity and various forms of mental illness. However, this does not explain the manifestations of supernatural strength recorded about the demoniac of Gadara; nor does it explain the references to lying spirits, familiar spirits—and most important to our study—spirits of affliction. Spirits of affliction, those spirits which manifest themselves through physical symptoms often similar to natural disease and injury, cannot be explained away as mental illness.

The hallucinations of Hollywood horror-mongers have made many leery of addressing the reality of demon spirits. Nevertheless, evil spirits do exist and seek to torment and oppress. We need to resist ridiculous imaginations of red eyes and green vomit when considering a confrontation with spirits of darkness. Save these exaggerations for the next *Exorcist* sequel. What we need is a Biblical battle plan of closing the door to every possible avenue of attack.

One reason I'm so passionate about the subject of spirits of affliction is because of my own experience. At the age of eight, I was having trouble with what appeared to be the onset of asthma. Several times while playing, it became difficult to breathe. I would wheeze and twice I actually passed out. My parents took me to the emergency room and then to our family physician. The doctor gave me an asthma starter kit that included information and an inhaler. More tests were planned, but the Lord had a different plan.

My father is a Pentecostal preacher of the highest order. The Painesville Revival Center, as it was called back then, was a great church to be raised in. At the risk of sounding too nostalgic, the Revival Center is where I came to know the Lord, was filled with the Holy Spirit, and met the love of my life. The Center also was a place where the Word was preached and signs and wonders were witnessed. On this particular Sunday night, the Reverend June Seabolt was preaching. She is a true-blue, dyed-in-the-wool woman of God. No one could ever accuse her of backing away from a demon. She called me to the front and, without knowing anything about my breathing trouble, began ministering to me. She said the enemy had sent an evil spirit to attack my lungs because God was going to use my voice for His glory. She rebuked the spirit of affliction and I can testify to being without a respiratory incident since then.

An important part of confronting illness and disease is to understand that sometimes it is rooted in a direct attack of the enemy. That is why there is a gift of the Holy Spirit called discernment of spirits.

"To another the working of miracles; to another prophecy; to another discerning of spirits; to another divers kinds of tongues; to another the interpretation of tongues:"

1 Corinthians 12:1

This is an important, often overlooked gift of the Spirit. The Lord is interested in giving us specific direction concerning our prayers. There is a sense of the Lord's frustration when we read the words written by James:

> *". . . You fight and war. Yet you do not have because you do not ask. You ask and do not receive, because you ask amiss, . . ."*

> **James 4:2-3 (NKJV)**

The gift of discernment exists so that we know how to pray, because we know what we are praying against. If you are dealing with a demon of affliction the Holy Spirit can and will expose it. What you will find when you confront the devil is that the Word is true.

> *"(For the weapons of our warfare are not carnal, but mighty through God to the pulling down of strong holds;)"*

> **2 Corinthians 10:4**

The power of God is overwhelming to the enemy. Don't fall prey to the "Star Wars" theology that equal and opposite powers must be kept in balance. This is Eastern mysticism, ying and yang.[2] This theology and mysticism is not the reality of true spiritual warfare. Our God is omnipotent and all-powerful. He is not Satan's opposite. God is superior in every way. If you will take your authority in the name of Jesus Christ, the enemy must acquiesce.

You are building a reputation in the realm of the spirit whether you know it or not.

> *"And the evil spirit answered and said, Jesus I know, and Paul I know; but who are ye? And*

the man in whom the evil spirit was leaped on them, and overcame them, and prevailed against them, so that they fled out of that house naked and wounded."

Acts 19:15-16

Demons are real, but so is the power of the Holy Spirit that is in you.

The part of this story which fascinates me is in verse fifteen: *". . . Paul I know; but who are ye? . . ."* You and I can literally build a reputation among evil spirits. Exercise your authority over every demonic influence in your life. Demons are real, but so is the power of the Holy Spirit that is in you.

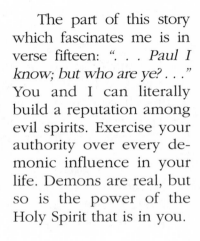

Scripture Meditations

"Ye are of God, little children, and have over-come them: because greater is he that is in you, than he that is in the world."

1 John 4:4

"When Jesus saw that the people came running together, he rebuked the foul spirit, saying unto him, Thou dumb and deaf spirit, I charge thee, come out of him, and enter no more into him."

Mark 9:25

"And they came over unto the other side of the sea, into the country of the Gadarenes. And when he was come out of the ship, immediately there met him out of the tombs a man with an unclean spirit, Who had his dwelling among the tombs; and no man could bind him, no, not with chains: Because that he had been often bound with fetters and chains, and the chains had been plucked asunder by him, and the fetters broken in pieces: neither could any man tame him. And always, night and day, he was in the mountains, and in the tombs, crying, and cutting himself with stones. But when he saw Jesus afar off, he ran and worshipped him, And cried with a loud voice, and said, What have I to do with thee, Jesus, thou Son of the most high God? I adjure thee by God, that

thou torment me not. For he said unto him, Come out of the man, thou unclean spirit. And he asked him, What is thy name? And he answered, saying, My name is Legion: for we are many. And he besought him much that he would not send them away out of the country. Now there was there nigh unto the mountains a great herd of swine feeding. And all the devils besought him, saying, Send us into the swine, that we may enter into them. And forthwith Jesus gave them leave. And the unclean spirits went out, and entered into the swine: and the herd ran violently down a steep place into the sea, (they were about two thousand;) and were choked in the sea. And they that fed the swine fled, and told it in the city, and in the country. And they went out to see what it was that was done. And they come to Jesus, and see him that was possessed with the devil, and had the legion, sitting, and clothed, and in his right mind: and they were afraid."

Mark 5:1-16

"And, behold, there was a woman which had a spirit of infirmity eighteen years, and was bowed together, and could in no wise lift up herself. And when Jesus saw her, he called her to him, and said unto her, Woman, thou art loosed from thine infirmity. And he laid his hands on her: and immediately she was made straight, and glorified God."

Luke 13:11-13

"And Jesus went about all Galilee, teaching in their synagogues, and preaching the gospel of the

kingdom, and healing all manner of sickness and all manner of disease among the people. And his fame went throughout all Syria: and they brought unto him all sick people that were taken with divers diseases and torments, and those which were possessed with devils, and those which were lunatick, and those that had the palsy; and he healed them."

Matthew 4:23-24

"When the even was come, they brought unto him many that were possessed with devils: and he cast out the spirits with his word, and healed all that were sick:"

Matthew 8:16

"These twelve Jesus sent forth, and commanded them, saying, Go not into the way of the Gentiles, and into any city of the Samaritans enter ye not: But go rather to the lost sheep of the house of Israel. And as ye go, preach, saying, The kingdom of heaven is at hand. Heal the sick, cleanse the lepers, raise the dead, cast out devils: freely ye have received, freely give."

Matthew 10:5-8

"And at even, when the sun did set, they brought unto him all that were diseased, and them that were possessed with devils. And all the city was gathered together at the door. And he healed many that were sick of divers diseases, and cast

out many devils; and suffered not the devils to speak, because they knew him."

Mark 1:32-34

"And these signs shall follow them that believe; In my name shall they cast out devils ; they shall speak with new tongues; They shall take up serpents; and if they drink any deadly thing, it shall not hurt them; they shall lay hands on the sick, and they shall recover."

Mark 16:17-18

"And certain women, which had been healed of evil spirits and infirmities, Mary called Magdalene, out of whom went seven devils,"

Luke 8:2

Fervent Prayer

"Confess your faults one to another, and pray
one for another, that ye may be healed.
The effectual fervent prayer of a righteous man
availeth much."

James 5:16

Often, in our thirst for revelation and under-standing, we neglect the obvious and direct approach—to offer up an impassioned petition, an effectual fervent prayer for divine inter-vention. We must, with increasingly importance, consider the significance of fervent prayer. The shortest distance between two points is a straight line and the direct approach is typically the best approach. Sometimes you just have to ask.

Is there such a thing as desperate faith? Some might argue that it is impossible to be filled with faith and desperation concerning any one thing. However, I don't agree with this presumption. Circumstances can be desperate, though our faith is constant. The idea that we are going to respond to life's troubles with a "yawn of faith" is denial of our humanity. The Lord understands we are creatures of emotion. After all, He created us this way. God isn't disturbed by our emotions. Our passion is not strange to Him. If we look through the Word of God, we will find our Heavenly Father is very passionate. Our God's emotional spectrum runs from hot red to placid blue, from righteous rage to amazing love.

Don't be among those who believe that if they manifest any emotion then they have surely lost all credibility with God. The enemy tricks us into believing that if we cry or wrestle with our joy that we have no faith or right to receive anything of the Lord. This is the wrong picture; it is not God's perspective.

True faith in no way operates in denial of reality.

"But he, being full of compassion, forgave their iniquity, and destroyed them not: yea, many a time turned he his anger away, and did not stir up all his wrath. For he remembered that they were but flesh; a wind that passeth away, and cometh not again."

Psalm 78:38-39

The Lord knows where we are coming from. Who would not question the sincerity of someone who is suffering in his or her body or burying a loved one and does not show a certain amount of consternation?

Faith is, first and foremost, honest and pure. James tells us to, *". . . ask in faith, nothing wavering. For he that wavereth is like a wave of the sea driven with the wind and tossed. For let not that man think that he shall receive anything of the Lord,"* (James 1:6-7).

True faith in no way operates in denial of reality. Some religions teach that one must deny reality to receive anything supernatural. This approach is occultic and anti-scriptural.

If you are hit by a bus, you can deny all you want that you're not hurting, but it won't change your situation. Your belief must be rooted in the Word of God and how that it speaks into your situation. Believing God is with you and will heal you is a long way from saying you being hit by the bus never happened. Walking in faith is not leaving your reality, but rather welcoming God's miraculous hand to move in the midst of your reality.

Just as you need not deny reality, you do not need to deny your emotions. Don't waste your passion on your problem; direct it towards your solution—Jesus Christ. The Lord is able to tell when someone who is desperate reaches out to touch Him.

"And Jesus said, Who touched me? When all denied, Peter and they that were with him said, Master, the multitude throng thee and press thee, and sayest thou, Who touched me? And Jesus said, Somebody hath touched me: for I perceive that virtue is gone out of me."

Luke 8:45-46

This woman was desperate. She had exhausted every avenue she could possibly think of. Maybe you can relate because you've spent large sums of money on various cures that have failed. What overwhelming disappointment this woman must have felt. But, hope began to blossom into faith when she said within herself, "If I can but touch the hem of His garment."

"When she had heard of Jesus, came in the press behind, and touched his garment. For she said, If I may touch but his clothes, I shall be whole."

Mark 5:27-28

There is something very special about learning to target all of our hopes and expectations upon the Lord.

Blind Bartimaeus cried out to Jesus, "Have mercy!"[1] When they told him to stop, he cried even louder. There was no doubt a great deal of emotion involved in such a persistent plea. His desperation, as well as that of the woman with blood issues, gained the Master's full attention. Don't measure your faith by how much you cry, but rather to whom you cry.

Remember the phrase "effectual fervent prayer"? In the original Greek, "effectual" is "energeo," pronounced "en-erg-eh'-o." *Strong's Concordance* gives us the following definitions: "to be operative, be at work; put forth power."[2] This describes the woman with the issue of blood and blind Bartimaeus. They put their desperation on display and every effort into reaching the Lord. Prayer is our way of reaching out and crying out for the help and healing of the Lord. Don't be ashamed to cry out to God. David said in Psalm 5:2: *"Hearken unto the voice of my cry, my King, and my God: for unto thee will I pray."*

Sometimes words are limited and faith decrees seem too mechanical to express your heartache, but God hears the voice in your cry and speaks the language of your tears. Your Heavenly Father will embrace you and bring comfort and resolution to your pain.

Scripture Meditations

"In my distress I called upon the LORD, and cried unto my God: he heard my voice out of his temple, and my cry came before him, even into his ears."

Psalm 18:6

"O Lord my God, I cried unto thee, and thou hast healed me."

Psalm 30:2

"And the children of Israel said to Samuel, Cease not to cry unto the LORD our God for us, that he will save us out of the hand of the Philistines."

1 Samuel 7:8

"And when we cried unto the LORD God of our fathers, the LORD heard our voice, and looked on our affliction, and our labour, and our oppression:"

Deuteronomy 26:7

"And he cried, saying, Jesus, thou Son of David, have mercy on me. And they which went before

rebuked him, that he should hold his peace: but he cried so much the more, Thou Son of David, have mercy on me. And Jesus stood, and commanded him to be brought unto him: and when he was come near, he asked him, Saying, What wilt thou that I shall do unto thee? And he said, Lord, that I may receive my sight. And Jesus said unto him, Receive thy sight: thy faith hath saved thee. And immediately he received his sight, and followed him, glorifying God: and all the people, when they saw it, gave praise unto God."

Luke 18: 38-43

"Likewise the Spirit also helpeth our infirmities: for we know not what we should pray for as we ought: but the Spirit itself maketh intercession for us with groanings which cannot be uttered."

Romans 8:26

Don't Confuse Your Faith with the Facts

"Through faith we understand that the worlds
were framed by the word of God, so that
things which are seen were not made of
things which do appear."

Hebrews 11:3

Your faith is your spiritual sight. We walk by faith and not by sight (2 Corinthians 5:7). Abraham, the father of faith, had far-reaching sight; he saw our day and rejoiced. Imagine what it was like for Abraham to rejoice way back then over what God is doing now. It may be a little strange to us, but not to him because he could see with his spiritual eyes. Learning to see in the spirit and, more importantly, *trusting* in what you see in the spirit is a major key to receiving your miracle.

Don't confuse your faith with the facts. To isolate this Satanic pothole on the road to your healing, you must discern between reality and perception. Most people only believe what they can see, hear, taste, smell, or feel. This is the limited reality most people are born with and die in. Missouri is the "Show Me State." You may or may not live in Missouri, but you probably live your life based solely on what you see. The truth is, what you can see, hear, taste, smell, or feel is not reality, but merely your perception of reality. Now, I don't want to lose anyone here by sounding too existential so I need to break this down a little further.

Most people have seen a magic show, either at a neighbor's birthday party or on television. Magicians are masters at creating wrong perception. Many an innocent rabbit has disappeared into a black silk top hat only to reappear moments later. On a much grander scale, jumbo jets have disappeared in front of millions on television specials. Did the rabbit or the jet truly disappear? No, but we perceived their disappearance with our sight. Truth be told, our sight is easily manipulated into false assumptions.

The Bible reveals how easily the senses can be tricked in the story of Jacob and Esau.

> *"And Jacob said unto his father, I am Esau thy firstborn; I have done according as thou badest me: arise, I pray thee, sit and eat of my venison, that thy soul may bless me."*

> **Genesis 27:19**

Jacob and his mother were very careful to exploit the perception of Isaac's aged senses.

We've all heard the expression that if it looks like a duck and it quacks like a duck and it waddles like a duck, then it's a duck. This illustrates our utter dependence upon our five senses for any and all confirmation of reality. This makes it very difficult for us to be transformed into Spirit-led believers. The Word says trust not in those things that are seen for they are temporal and will pass away. Trust, rather, in those things which are unseen; for those things are eternal and will never pass away. There is an unseen world around us that is more real, more permanent, and more accessible than many of us realize. This world is that fifth dimension. Your miracle healing already exists in this dimension and you need a plan to go in and extract your blessing and deposit it into your tangible world.

Some will never admit this world exists when others will do everything they can to contact this fifth dimension. America and the world's fascination with this unseen world has led to the present-day popularity of psychics, mediums, astrology, meditation, New Age, and Eastern philosophy. If life is nothing more than living and dying and paying bills, then why is the world so desperate to touch this unseen world? Even lost souls of this world search by using drastic measures to connect to a spiritual realm they instinctively know exists.

Perhaps the most exiting thing about the Christian perspective of the fifth dimension is that God has called us to "walk in the Spirit." Did you catch that? Not to visit or dabble or contact momentarily or once in a life time experience, but the Lord has called us to walk in the Spirit every day. Let's take a moment and look at the life of Christ and see to what extent Christ moved in this fifth dimension.

Far too many believers want to contact the fifth dimension but not live there. I would like to say something here without offending anyone. God did not call us to go to church; He called you to be the church. Most of our churches are structured to match the spiritual lives of the membership. We visit church

Real church is not an event; it is an experience.

twice a week and dip our big toe in the realm of the super-natural and very quickly, usually before the dismissal prayer, we return to the carnal, fleshly realm we live in. Don't you understand? Your environment has nothing to do with your proximity to God? Real church is not an event; it is an experience. A new birth. A baptism of fire. Real church is not singing three fast songs and two slow songs and hearing a so-called sermon with three points and a poem, then returning to "life." Church is the place where we are charged up, stirred up, and equipped to *"go into all the world and preach the Gospel,"* (Mark 16:15). That includes your world.

God is looking for people who want more than a visitation of His presence. He desires people who want the habitation of His presence. God didn't call you to *visit* the Spirit, but to *walk* in the Spirit.

"For as many as are led by the Spirit of God, they are the sons of God."

Romans 8:14

Many of today's Christians have set their sights on the low call, dancing over the brass having never seen the gold. Christ began at a very young age to stand out as someone quite special. At the age of twelve, we see Him being left behind the caravan because He said, *"Wist ye not that I must be about* my *Father's business,"* (Luke 2:49). Walking in the Spirit has nothing to do with your age.

Samuel was only a child when he heard the voice of Lord calling to him at bedtime (1 Samuel 3:6-10). When you are truly walking in the fifth dimension, your life, and even everyday events will carry with them an overwhelming sense of destiny and purpose. How sad is it that so many people live their entire lives feeling very small and insignificant because they haven't discovered their eternal purpose.

In the story of the woman at the well in John 4, Christ said to His disciples in verse 32, *"I have meat to eat that you know not."* The disciples thought He spoke of lunch because they were looking through natural eyes and being led by carnal appetites. Christ said, "My meat is to do the will of the Father who sent me," (see John 4:34).

Do you have a hunger and desire to walk in the fifth dimension? That desire was put there by God and cries out for more than the mundane Pentecostal potluck of food, fun, and fellowship.

> **"Deep calleth unto deep at the noise of thy waterspouts: all thy waves and thy billows are gone over me."**
>
> **Psalm 42:7**

This desire left unfulfilled can become a source of great sorrow.

> **"Hope deferred maketh the heart sick: but when the desire cometh, it is a tree of life."**
>
> **Proverbs 13:12**

I have often felt the frustration of attempting to accomplish something for the kingdom with human effort. That effort always falls short of the glory. Many good things are done by well-meaning people, but nothing is a worthy substitute for the Holy Spirit.

Unfathomable excess and foolishness has turned many away from their desire to walk in the Spirit. We should not look to the self-appointed apostles of this age for our example when Christ and His apostles have already blazoned a trail into this dimension. I don't want to get too far into this topic of walking in the fifth dimension, but you must learn to trust the unseen world around you.

> *"While we look not at the things which are seen, but at the things which are not seen: for the things which are seen are temporal; but the things which are not seen are eternal."*

> **2 Corinthians 4:18**

Don't allow those who teach out of balance and without proper Biblical reference to turn you away from your divine purpose. The Lord has called you to walk in the Spirit.

The reason so many of today's Christians cannot overcome habits and addictions is because we are living by our senses. This also explains why divorce is as rampant in the Church as it is in the world. You are not a *body*-being; you are a *spirit*-being. Your eternal future is being held in jeopardy because of your inability to overcome this rudimentary carnal plane of existence. I hope you can now see that the modern Christian weakness toward sin is directly related to his/her inability to walk in the Spirit.

"This I say then, Walk in the Spirit, and ye shall not fulfil the lust of the flesh."

Galatians 5:16

Walk in the Spirit and you will not succumb to the lust of the flesh. Your victory over the flesh is in your willingness and desire to walk in the Spirit. Most of us don't want to think too hard about where we may be falling short of the glory of God. Can you think of a more depressing subject? We have little in the way of excuses; for the Word says, *"There hath no temptation taken you but such as is common to man: but God is faithful, who will not suffer you to be tempted above that ye are able; but will with the temptation also make a way to escape, that ye may be able to bear it,"* (1 Corinthians 10:13).

We are missing out on our health, prosperity, and power. You won't find them in this carnal plane, but they are already yours in the Spirit. What you may call the facts are merely your perceptions. Satan will go out of his way to paint a portrait through circumstance that is in stark opposition to God's promises. It's time to move beyond our natural senses and listen with our spiritual ears. You are blessed and highly favored of the Lord. You are more than a conqueror through Christ. By His stripes you are healed. Don't let the devil confuse your faith with the facts. You are what God says you are. You have what God says you have. You can do what God says you can do.

Take time to read these few verses and remember it is by the Word of God that the worlds were framed.

Scripture Meditations

"(As it is written, I have made thee a father of many nations,) before him whom he believed, even God, who quickeneth the dead, and calleth those things which be not as though they were. Who against hope believed in hope, that he might become the father of many nations, according to that which was spoken, So shall thy seed be. And being not weak in faith, he considered not his own body now dead, when he was about an hundred years old, neither yet the deadness of Sara's womb: He staggered not at the promise of God through unbelief; but was strong in faith, giving glory to God; And being fully persuaded that, what he had promised, he was able also to perform."

Romans 4:17-21

"By faith Noah, being warned of God of things not seen as yet, moved with fear, prepared an ark to the saving of his house; by the which he condemned the world, and became heir of the righteousness which is by faith. By faith Abraham, when he was called to go out into a place which he should after receive for an inheritance, obeyed; and he went out, not knowing whither he went."

Hebrews 11:7-8

"These all died in faith, not having received the promises, but having seen them afar off, and were persuaded of them, and embraced them, and confessed that they were strangers and pilgrims on the earth."

Hebrews 11:13

"By faith he forsook Egypt, not fearing the wrath of the king: for he endured, as seeing him who is invisible."

Hebrews 11:27

"Jesus saith unto him, Thomas, because thou hast seen me, thou hast believed: blessed are they that have not seen, and yet have believed."

John 20:29

"For by him were all things created, that are in heaven, and that are in earth, visible and invisible, whether they be thrones, or dominions, or principalities, or powers: all things were created by him, and for him"

Colossians 1:16

DAY 10

Healing Forgiveness

"When you forgive this man, I forgive him, too.
And when I forgive him (for whatever is to be forgiven),
I do so with Christ's authority for your benefit,"

2 Corinthians 2:10 (NLT)

One of the great lessons of life is learning how to let go. We tend to hang onto things—good and bad. Many of us can best be described as "emotional pack rats." I don't know about you, but I've got report cards from thirty years ago. I have a hard time letting go of things sometimes. We must face the inevitable need to let go of our past in order to make room for our present. Now is the time to set free the lava lamps and moods rings.

This is important to your health as well. Past emotional and spiritual hurts turn into present-day physical hurts. A sick soul will make a sick body. Poisoned arrows of offense and unforgiveness will stop the miracle-working power of God from flowing into your life.

***"Your heavenly Father will forgive you if you
forgive those who sin against you; but if you***

refuse to forgive them, he will not forgive you.

Matthew 6:14 (TLB)

All healing flows from the cross. If you have separated yourself from Christ then there is not hope for your soul or body.

Selwyn Hughes was an evangelical preacher whose devotionals entitled "Everyday with Jesus" had a readership of over one million around the world. He writes:

"An unforgiving spirit is one of the biggest contributors towards physical and emotional ill health."[1]

This quote illustrates the potential dangers to your physical health that unforgiveness brings. There is an undeniable link between an aching heart and an aching body. Forgiveness is more important to the forgiver than the forgiven. As long as you are holding onto a grudge you cannot be healed. When we have been hurt or offended, we tend to keep on telling our side, defending ourselves to anyone that will listen. Did you ever stop to think that if you are defending yourself to someone then, in essence, you have made them your judge? You see, it's not until we release our rights that God can assume His rightful place as judge.

Many of us have a fundamental misunderstanding of what forgiveness is. In our present culture, when someone says, "I'm sorry," we respond, "It's okay." This can cause trouble when we have been truly wronged by someone. How do you tell someone who was abused or who molested you, "It's okay,"?

It's *not* okay nor will it ever be okay! But, true forgiveness is not saying, "It's okay." Forgiveness simply means, "You owe me nothing." You are saying that you aren't going to hold onto this until they do the right thing. You forgive. You can forgive someone, and then it is up to the Lord—and sometimes even the courts—to hand out any justice. That is no longer your responsibility. "I forgive" doesn't mean that it's okay. It doesn't mean the offender won't face the law or have to face God for himself. Saying you forgive someone just means they don't owe you anything, including reasons or justification. Unforgiveness holds on to the hurt and pain and keeps it constantly stirred up so that when the offender comes to make it right, then it is still there to be made right. The *real* problem is that not everyone is going to come to you and make it right.

> Forget about who is wrong. Get the poison out of your spirit before it kills you.

We must forgive those who have offended us and release them into heaven's court. As long as we are hanging onto bitterness, the Lord cannot deal with the situation. Our miracle may be held up as the Lord waits for us to offer our forgiveness.

> **"Then said Jesus, Father, forgive them; for they know not what they do . . ."**
>
> **Luke 23:34**

More compassionate and selfless words have ever been spoken. This is why death could not hold Christ's body in the ground. Christ was right and yet He claimed no rights for Himself. Too often, the Church chooses rightness over righteousness. Forget about who is right and who is wrong. Get the poison out of your spirit before it kills you.

A beaten, bruised, and battered Christ made no defense. This is why death had to relinquish any claim on the Lord Jesus.

"O death, where is thy sting? O grave, where is thy victory? The sting of death is sin; and the strength of sin is the law. But thanks be to God, which giveth us the victory through our Lord Jesus Christ."

1 Corinthians 15:55-57

The path to the resurrection power of Christ goes, first, through the cross, "Father, forgive."[2]

"But if the Spirit of him that raised up Jesus from the dead dwell in you, he that raised up Christ from the dead shall also quicken your mortal bodies by his Spirit that dwelleth in you."

Romans 8:11

Bitterness is the poison we drink while waiting for someone else to die. Visit, call, or write to the person who has offended you. Don't offer explanations and defenses just extend your sincere forgiveness. Whether they respond or not is not relevant. You will be the benefactor.

Dr. Lewis Smedes was a prolific Christian author whose most famous book was entitled, "Forgive and Forget."[3] He says:

> *"The first and often the only person to be healed by forgiveness is the person who does the forgiveness. . . . When we genuinely forgive, we set a prisoner free and then discover that the prisoner we set free was us."*

Scripture Meditations

"So shall ye say unto Joseph, Forgive, I pray thee now, the trespass of thy brethren, and their sin; for they did unto thee evil: and now, we pray thee, forgive the trespass of the servants of the God of thy father. And Joseph wept when they spake unto him. And his brethren also went and fell down before his face; and they said, Behold, we be thy servants. And Joseph said unto them, Fear not: for am I in the place of God?"

Genesis 50:17-19

"Then came Peter to him, and said, Lord, how oft shall my brother sin against me, and I forgive him? till seven times? Jesus saith unto him, I say not unto thee, Until seven times: but, Until seventy times seven. Therefore is the kingdom of heaven likened unto a certain king, which would take account of his servants. And when he had begun to reckon, one was brought unto him, which owed him ten thousand talents. But forasmuch as he had not to pay, his lord commanded him to be sold, and his wife, and children, and all that he had, and payment to be made. The servant therefore fell down, and worshipped him, saying, Lord, have patience with me, and I will pay thee all. Then the lord of that servant was moved with compassion, and loosed him, and forgave him the debt. But the same servant went out, and found one of his fellowser-

vants, which owed him an hundred pence: and he laid hands on him, and took him by the throat, saying, Pay me that thou owest. And his fellowservant fell down at his feet, and besought him, saying, Have patience with me, and I will pay thee all. And he would not: but went and cast him into prison, till he should pay the debt. So when his fellowservants saw what was done, they were very sorry, and came and told unto their lord all that was done. Then his lord, after that he had called him, said unto him, O thou wicked servant, I forgave thee all that debt, because thou desiredst me: Shouldest not thou also have had compassion on thy fellowservant, even as I had pity on thee? And his lord was wroth, and delivered him to the tormentors, till he should pay all that was due unto him. So likewise shall my heavenly Father do also unto you, if ye from your hearts forgive not every one his brother their trespasses."

Matthew 18:21-35

"Grudge not one against another, brethren, lest ye be condemned: behold, the judge standeth before the door. . . . Is any among you afflicted? Let him pray. Is any merry? Let him sing psalms. Is any sick among you? Let him call for the elders of the church; and let them pray over him, anointing him with oil in the name of the Lord: And the prayer of faith shall save the sick, and the Lord shall raise him up; and if he have committed sins, they shall be forgiven him. Confess your faults one to another, and pray one for another, that ye may be healed. The effectual fervent prayer of a righteous man availeth much."

James 5:9, 13-16

"Put on therefore, as the elect of God, holy and beloved, bowels of mercies, kindness, humbleness of mind, meekness, longsuffering; Forbearing one another, and forgiving one another, if any man have a quarrel against any: even as Christ forgave you, so also do ye. And above all these things put on charity, which is the bond of perfectness. And let the peace of God rule in your hearts, to the which also ye are called in one body; and be ye thankful."

Colossians 3:12-15

DAY 11

Prescription Music

"But now bring me a minstrel. And it came to pass, when the minstrel played, that the hand of the LORD came upon him."

2 Kings 3:15

Music takes an express flight to the soul. There is no question something is very spiritual about music. More than once I have felt the soothing power of a song pull me up out of depression. Music and mood seem to go hand-in-hand. The right music can lift your faith, lighten your burden, and even set the tone for more intimate devotion. Music doesn't just speak to the heart; music gets in your head and stays there.

Who can forget the jingle: "Here's the story, of a man named Brady . . ."? *Please, Lord, make it stop!* For me, there must be a reason I remember all the words to the *Spider-Man* cartoon theme song from the early 1970s. Perhaps it's the repetition, or maybe it's one of those left-brain versus right-brain things. Whatever the cause, the effect is too powerful to ignore. The music we listen to repeatedly becomes a permanent part of us.

This should make us very cautious about what music we expose ourselves to on a regular basis. The old joke about the guy who played a country music record backwards comes to mind. Supposedly he got his job back, his wife back, and his dog came home.

Does depressing music cause depression? I don't know, but it certainly invites the depression to take its shoes off and sit for a spell. Retailers conduct major research to select the right music to put us in a buying mood. Employers select the music that increases productivity. These subtle, musical influences can have a profound effect on everything from our buying habits to our love life.

"The Love Boat promises something for everyone."[1] Okay, that's the last one of those. I promise. But, we should acknowledge the impact of music and enact a plan for building our faith.

Praise the Lord for the worship revolution of the past few years. Most contemporary Christian artists are focusing on worship now and are producing some of the most exciting and intimate songs ever. Empower yourself with music that lifts you up, challenges you to worship, and strengthens your faith.

There is so much in the Bible about praise and worship that is worth studying, but let's focus on just a few points. First, is the story of King Jehoshaphat and how the Lord told him to send Judah first and the battle would be won.[2] Judah simply means "praise." Send up the praise first and the battle will be won. This is kind of backwards from how we approach most battles. We wait for the victory and then offer up the praise. This makes our praise seem less genuine and, quite frankly, more similar to a *Price is Right* announcer saying, "It's a new car!" God wants our praise to be proactive, not reactive. You may be in the greatest battle of your life, but I encourage you to send Judah first so your battle may be won.

Second, let's look at a ruddy, shepherd boy named David. What a songster and a warrior. Those things do seem to run together in Scripture. King Saul was definitely falling away from the Lord, so much so that he was tormented by evil spirits.

> *"But the Spirit of the LORD departed from Saul, and an evil spirit from the LORD troubled him."*
>
> **1 Samuel 16:14**

Word came to Saul concerning David's skill with the harp and young David was invited to play for the king. Imagine King Saul trying to ease his tortured mind and young David playing his harp and singing in Hebrew the twenty-third Psalm. *"The LORD is my shepherd; I shall not want. He maketh me to lie down in green pastures: he leadeth me beside the still waters. He restoreth my soul: . . ."* The Psalms are so beautiful when read; we easily forget that it is a songbook. The demon powers that troubled King Saul had to leave as David worshipped the Good Shepherd. The atmosphere of demonic depression was changed by anointed music.

> *"And it came to pass, when the evil spirit from God was upon Saul, that David took an harp, and played with his hand: so Saul was refreshed, and was well, and the evil spirit departed from him."*
>
> **1 Samuel 16:23**

Sometimes even our own home can become a depressing place. Bad memories of disappointment and arguments can color our feelings toward our surroundings. Once joyful echoes of family, holidays, and friends can become moans of regret and cries of desperation. Anointed music can and will change the atmosphere. You can set the tone or mood of your day by surrounding your devotional time with anointed music that magnifies the Lord. If you ask someone what it means to magnify something most might say, without thinking, that it makes things bigger. But truthfully, to magnify something doesn't make it bigger; it only enlarges your perception. God is already big enough to fill the vastness of space and time but sometimes our perception of God is so small. When we magnify the Lord, our perception changes and we get a closer look at how truly awesome and powerful our God is. Select songs that sing of the Lord's greatness.

When we magnify the Lord, our perception changes and we get a closer look at how truly awesome and powerful our God is.

"Great is the LORD, and greatly to be praised; and his greatness is unsearchable."

Psalm 145:3

This will magnify God and multiply your faith. Anointed music ushers in the presence of the Lord.

Find those Christian artists that are more than just good musicians and singers. Find true worshippers who pour themselves out before the Lord. If you feel like an artist is singing *to you*, then keep looking until you find that special someone who is singing to the Lord. You're looking for someone who expresses your heart toward God. This is the background of your devotion. They cannot praise for you but they can lead you into your own time of worship before the throne.

Devotional music is not the only place you can use the tremendous power of music. Set as a backdrop to work and travel time, I suggest you select something which builds your faith. Songs that speak directly about Jehovah Rapha's healing power and songs that celebrate the miracle-working power of God can make the difference in your faith.

I attended my first Pentecostal revival service when I was three days old. I have been to many miracle services, even a few under the old gospel tents. What an era of miracle revivals the Lord sent in the fifties and sixties. Unfortunately, I just caught the tail end of the healing revivals. One thing I will never forget is getting under the gospel tent of R.W. Shambach in Cleveland, Ohio. Only a small boy, I still remember the music that filled the tent. Songs like: "Leave it There," "Are You Ready for a Miracle?" and "I Got Just What I Wanted from the Lord," just to name a few. By the time the preacher had preached and the choir had sung, you believed the Lord could do anything in that place on that night.

My mother is a Godly woman who has stood by my father's side through forty years of ministry. When someone in my father's church suffered a serious attack of Gilliam Bar Syndrome (GBS), they told this person she would never walk again. My mother felt impressed of the Holy Spirit to put a tape together of healing songs and take the tape along with a cassette player to the hospital. Several weeks passed and this victim of GBS listened to this tape for hours on end. One song on the tape entitled,

"Rise and Walk," was written by my good friend Mike Payne. He puts himself in the place of the lame man at the gate called Beautiful. As the song progresses, the miracle recorded in Acts is recounted in great detail. The final line is, "I can walk, hallelujah I can walk, hallelujah and all the glory I give unto the Lord." Those words spoke faith to the woman and she felt God was speaking directly to her situation through that song. She went into physical therapy and in a few months, against all odds, she walked into my father's church and shared the testimony of how the Lord had given her back the full use of her legs. She is still healed and walking around today preaching the Gospel. Anointed music may hold the key to your miracle healing.

Scripture Meditations

"Then believed they his words; they sang his praise."

Psalm 106:12

"And it came to pass, when the evil spirit from God was upon Saul, that David took an harp, and played with his hand: so Saul was refreshed, and was well, and the evil spirit departed from him."

1 Samuel 16:23

"And the evil spirit from the LORD was upon Saul, as he sat in his house with his javelin in his hand: and David played with his hand. And Saul sought to smite David even to the wall with the javelin; but he slipped away out of Saul's presence, and he smote the javelin into the wall: and David fled, and escaped that night."

1 Samuel 19:9-10

"In that day shall this song be sung in the land of Judah; We have a strong city; salvation will God appoint for walls and bulwarks. Open ye the gates, that the righteous nation which keepeth the truth may enter in. Thou wilt keep him in perfect

peace, whose mind is stayed on thee: because he trusteth in thee. Trust ye in the LORD for ever: for in the LORD JEHOVAH is everlasting strength:"

Isaiah 26:1-4

"And when they began to sing and to praise, the LORD set ambushments against the children of Ammon, Moab, and mount Seir, which were come against Judah; and they were smitten."

2 Chronicles 20:22

"I will be glad and rejoice in thee: I will sing praise to thy name, O thou most High. When mine enemies are turned back, they shall fall and perish at thy presence."

Psalm 9:2-3

"I will sing unto the LORD as long as I live: I will sing praise to my God while I have my being. My meditation of him shall be sweet: I will be glad in the LORD."

Psalm 104:33-34

"It came even to pass, as the trumpeters and singers were as one, to make one sound to be heard in praising and thanking the LORD; and when they lifted up their voice with the trumpets and cymbals and instruments of musick, and praised the LORD, saying, For he is good; for his

mercy endureth for ever: that then the house was filled with a cloud, even the house of the LORD; So that the priests could not stand to minister by reason of the cloud: for the glory of the LORD had filled the house of God."

2 Chronicles 5:13-14

"And the son said unto him, Father, I have sinned against heaven, and in thy sight, and am no more worthy to be called thy son. But the father said to his servants, Bring forth the best robe, and put it on him; and put a ring on his hand, and shoes on his feet: And bring hither the fatted calf, and kill it; and let us eat, and be merry: For this my son was dead, and is alive again; he was lost, and is found. And they began to be merry. Now his elder son was in the field: and as he came and drew nigh to the house, he heard musick and dancing."

Luke 15:21-25

"And at midnight Paul and Silas prayed, and sang praises unto God: and the prisoners heard them. And suddenly there was a great earthquake, so that the foundations of the prison were shaken: and immediately all the doors were opened, and every one's bands were loosed."

Acts 16:25-26

"For this is my blood of the new testament, which is shed for many for the remission of sins. But I say unto you, I will not drink henceforth of this

fruit of the vine, until that day when I drink it new with you in my Father's kingdom. And when they had sung an hymn, they went out into the Mount of Olives."

Matthew 26:28-30

DAY 12

A Merry Heart

"A merry heart doeth good like a medicine:
but a broken spirit drieth the bones."

Proverbs 17:22

D id you know that the word "blessed" translated
in the King James Version of the Bible, literally
means "happy"?[1]

Take a fresh look at the Sermon on the Mount
found in Matthew chapter five.[2] Christ was very much
interested in our "happiness." Perhaps, many Christians
have missed this most important aspect of our daily
walk with Christ. I can only say that in the wake of all
the miserable Christians I have met over the years,
many have the appearance of someone just smacked
in the face with a dead rabbit.

The Lord did not come to bring you life and life
more depressing. An abundant life is a happy life. The
apostle, Paul, said in Philippians 4:11-13, *"Not that I
speak in respect of want: for I have learned, in
whatsoever state I am, therewith to be content. I know
both how to be abased, and I know how to abound:
every where and in all things I am instructed both to
be full and to be hungry, both to abound and to suffer*

need. I can do all things through Christ which strengtheneth me. Whether I abound or am abased . . ."

This is a picture of how trials are to be faced. Are your circumstances the determining factor when it comes to your sense of well-being and joy? True joy cannot be externally motivated. There are thrills and sensations that come with fun and good news. However, the kind of joy that is your strength is not a result of what happens to you but rather what happens in you. When you come to truly know the Lord in a real and personal way, there is a joy that can only be found in His presence.

". . . the kind of joy that is your strength is not a result of what happens to you but rather what happens in you."

I have never quite understood the American Christian's struggle with prayer. Having a daily time of devotion and prayer with the Lord is more refreshing than a shower and more fun than a round of golf. There is such a feeling of elation that accompanies the Lord's presence. Words are useless to describe the sensation. When you learn to enter into the Lord's presence daily, there is security and sense of wellness that is not contingent upon your bank balance or present physical condition. With our busy lives, it's so easy to be too busy to pray. Martin Luther said, "I have so much to do today that I should spend the first three hours in prayer."[3]

This way of looking at things is far removed from our twenty-first century view of prayer. Usually, prayer is the first thing we cut from our busy schedule.

Depression is best defined as absence from the presence of the Lord.

> *"Thou wilt shew me the path of life: in thy presence is fulness of joy; at thy right hand there are pleasures for evermore."*

Psalm 16:11

Coming daily into the Lord's presence is not only a cure for depression, but it is a pathway to true joy. Regardless of what you are battling in your body, your spirit can rejoice in the presence of the Lord.

Perhaps you have been subjected to a negative prognosis. Most people might wilt at the thought of facing your present condition. But, in the presence of the Lord, there is a sense of hope and joy that He Who sits on the throne is on your side. The closer we get to the Lord, the more His glory is revealed. This fact by itself is a tremendous source of joy. To realize just how big God is and how small our problems are, in comparison, is cause to rejoice.

Imagine being lost in the woods on the verge of nightfall. The evening shadows grow longer with each passing moment. Every tree and potential marker looks the same and fear begins to whisper, "All is lost." A chilling wind reminds you that the nights are cold in these mountains and you are ill-equipped to face it. "Crack!" A twig snaps in the near brush. "Snap!" There it is again. You crouch behind the nearest tree hoping the beast will just keep right on going. Then, you hear your name through the shadows. Am I hallucinating? Out of the dusk steps your rescuer, a uniformed park ranger. Hallelujah! I'm saved. Now, that would be a joyful feeling to realize that help is much closer than you ever imagined.

Well, I want you to know that no matter what forest of sickness or pain you are lost in, Jesus is as close as the mention of His Name. Call on the Lord and He will answer you. You, too will say, "Hallelujah, I'm saved."

When we realize we are no longer lost, then we will have a real sense of joy in our lives. No matter our circumstances, it's enough to know that "I once was lost but now I'm found; was blind but now I see."[4]

To know with great certainty that you have been born again is the real key to lasting joy. The old-timers called it a "blessed assurance." As we have already learned, that simply means "happy assurance." You are not alone.

Joy, when one learns to take hold of it and hang on to it has a tremendous healing power. The Word says that a merry heart doeth good like a medicine (Proverbs 17:22).

"A good laugh and a long sleep are the best cures in the doctor's book."

~Irish Proverb

"Laughter is a tranquilizer with no side effects."

~Arnold Glasow

"With the fearful strain that is on me night and day, if I did not laugh I should die."

~Abraham Lincoln

You should guard your joy for the sake of your health and healing.

Scripture Meditations

"Then he said unto them, Go your way, eat the fat, and drink the sweet, and send portions unto them for whom nothing is prepared: for this day is holy unto our LORD: neither be ye sorry; for the joy of the LORD is your strength."

Nehemiah 8:10

"Thou wilt shew me the path of life: in thy presence is fulness of joy; at thy right hand there are pleasures for evermore."

Psalm 16:11

"Sing unto the LORD, O ye saints of his, and give thanks at the remembrance of his holiness. For his anger endureth but a moment; in his favour is life: weeping may endure for a night, but joy cometh in the morning. And in my prosperity I said, I shall never be moved."

Psalm 30:4-6

"Be glad in the LORD, and rejoice, ye righteous: and shout for joy, all ye that are upright in heart."

Psalm 32:11

"My soul shall make her boast in the LORD: the humble shall hear thereof, and be glad."

Psalm 34:2

"But let the righteous be glad; let them rejoice before God: yea, let them exceedingly rejoice."

Psalm 68:3

"For the kingdom of God is not meat and drink; but righteousness, and peace, and joy in the Holy Ghost."

Romans 14:17

"Hope deferred maketh the heart sick: but when the desire cometh, it is a tree of life."

Proverbs 13:12

"My brethren, count it all joy when ye fall into divers temptations; Knowing this, that the trying of your faith worketh patience. But let patience have her perfect work, that ye may be perfect and entire, wanting nothing."

James 1:2-4

Day 13

Smith Wigglesworth

"Ye are of God, little children, and have overcome them: because greater is he that is in you, than he that is in the world."

1 John 4:4

Smith Wigglesworth, the great apostle of faith, was a true man of God. In an age when men of God are scrutinized in every minute detail, Wigglesworth stands out as a man above reproach. He went on to be with the Lord in 1947 at the age of eighty-seven. Even his death was a testimony because he passed on without suffering. A doctor's first-hand account described Wigglesworth as a perfect male who seemed to have finished a day's work and went to sleep.

Wigglesworth was a plumber by trade and had little formal education. His wife taught him to read at the age of twenty-six. He was a man taught by the Holy Spirit. Often, his blue-collar ministry approach was seen as gruff and unrefined, but no one can argue with the incredible testimonies from his ministry. Many incredible healings and creative miracles happened wherever Wigglesworth went. Here is a story Wigglesworth tells:

"I was called at ten o'clock one night to pray for a young person given up by the doctor who was dying of consumption. As I looked, I saw that unless God undertook it was impossible for her to live. I turned to the mother and said, 'Well, mother. You will have to go to bed.' She said, 'Oh, I have not had my clothes off for three weeks.' I said to the daughters, 'You will have to go to bed,' but they did not want to go. It was the same with the son. I put on my overcoat and said, 'Good-bye, I'm off.' They said, 'Oh, don't leave us.' I said, 'I can do nothing here.' They said, 'Oh, if you will stop, we will all go to bed.' I knew that God would move nothing in an atmosphere of mere natural sympathy and unbelief.

They all went to bed and I stayed, and that was surely a time as I knelt by that bed face to face with death and with the devil. But God can change the hardest situation and make you know that He is almighty.

Then the fight came. It seemed as though the heavens were brass. I prayed from 11 p.m. to 3:30 in the morning. I saw the glimmering light on the face of the sufferer and saw her pass away. The devil said, 'Now you are done for. You have come from Bradford and the girl has died on your hands.' I said, 'It can't be. God did not send me here for nothing. This is a time to change strength.' I remembered that passage which said, 'Men ought always to pray and not to faint.' Death had taken place but I knew that my God was all-powerful and He that had split the Red Sea is just the same today. It was a time when I would not have

'No,' and God said, 'Yes.' I looked at the window and at that moment the face of Jesus appeared. It seemed as though a million rays of light were coming from His face. As He looked at the one who had just passed away, the color came back to her face. She rolled over and fell asleep. Then I had a glorious time. In the morning she woke early, put on a dressing gown and walked to the piano. She started to play and to sing a wonderful song. The mother and the sister and the brother had all come down to listen. The Lord had undertaken. A miracle had been wrought."[1]

Some have called Smith Wigglesworth God's man of rough-and-tumble faith because at times Wigglesworth would hit people during prayer. For example, one woman had a stomach tumor and Wigglesworth suddenly punched her in the stomach. She was instantly healed. When Wigglesworth was asked why he hit people sometimes when praying for them. He said, "I don't hit people. I hit the devil. If they get in the way, I can't help it." He used to say, "You can't deal gently with the devil, nor comfort him; he likes comfort."

There is a real attempt today to complicate the process of faith for divine healing.

This man of faith pulled no punches when dealing with the devil. He believed and taught that sickness was from the devil and had to be dealt with by taking authority over the enemy. Many people might consider this approach too simplistic; but for Wigglesworth, it was the key to his amazing legacy of miracles.

There is a real attempt today to complicate the process of faith for divine healing. This can easily lead down a path to very religious sounding excuses that relinquish our faith. My friend and mentor is Bob Rogers, the pastor of one of America's great churches, Evangel World Prayer Center in Louisville Kentucky. If I have heard him say it once, I have heard it a thousand times: "God is a good God and the devil is a bad devil; everything good comes from God and everything bad comes from the devil." I believe Wigglesworth would agree.

There is an awesome story about Wigglesworth waking up in the middle of the night to see Satan sitting on the edge of his bed. Now, I'm not sure how you might respond to such a situation, but just the thought of it causes the hair on the back my neck to rise ever so slightly. Wigglesworth's response was not to scream out a vehement prayer or rebuke. Some of us might have tried to find a little holy water real quick. Wigglesworth simply said, "Oh, it's just you." Then he rolled over and went back to sleep. Perhaps this was a vision or a dream, but what is important is that we get a sense of the authority and confidence this man of God walked in.

Wigglesworth also said:

"There are some times when you pray for the sick and you are apparently rough. But you are not dealing with a person; you are dealing with the satanic forces that are binding the person. Your heart is full of love and compassion to all, but you are moved to a holy anger as you see

the place the devil has taken in the body of the sick one, and you deal with his position with a real forcefulness. One day a pet dog followed a lady out of her house and ran all round her feet. She said to the dog, 'My dear, I cannot have you with me today.' The dog wagged its tail and made a big fuss. She said, 'Go home, my dear.' But the dog did not go. At last she shouted roughly, 'GO HOME,' and off it went. Some people deal with the devil like that; the devil can stand all the comfort you like to give him. Cast him out! You are dealing not with the person; you are dealing with the devil. Demon power must be dislodged in the name of the Lord. You are always right when you dare to deal with sickness as with the devil. Much sickness is caused by some misconduct, there is something wrong, there is some neglect somewhere, and Satan has had a chance to get in. It is necessary to repent and confess where you have given place to the devil, and then he can be dealt with."[2]

You have absolute power over the devil in the name of Jesus Christ. The devil is *"seeking whom he may devour,"* (1 Peter 5:8). Have you ever wondered who those people are? You know, the ones "he may devour"? Maybe more important are the ones he may not devour?

Take your authority in Christ Jesus. *". . . Resist the devil, and he will flee . . . ,"* (James 4:7). You might be surprised at how quickly Satan must retreat and take his symptoms with him. Here's your chance to punch the devil in the gut. Draw the battle lines and declare war on sickness and pain!

Scripture Meditations

"The eternal God is thy refuge, and underneath are the everlasting arms: and he shall thrust out the enemy from before thee; and shall say, Destroy them."

Deuteronomy 33:27

"Submit yourselves therefore to God. Resist the devil, and he will flee from you."

James 4:7

"So shall they fear the name of the LORD from the west, and his glory from the rising of the sun. When the enemy shall come in like a flood, the Spirit of the LORD shall lift up a standard against him."

Isaiah 59:19

"Verily, verily, I say unto you, He that believeth on me, the works that I do shall he do also; and greater works than these shall he do; because I go unto my Father."

John 14:12

"For though we walk in the flesh, we do not war after the flesh: (For the weapons of our warfare are not carnal, but mighty through God to the pulling down of strong holds;)"

2 Corinthians 10:3-4

"These things speak, and exhort, and rebuke with all authority…"

Titus 2:15

"No weapon that is formed against thee shall prosper; and every tongue that shall rise against thee in judgment thou shalt condemn. This is the heritage of the servants of the LORD, and their righteousness is of me, saith the LORD."

Isaiah 54:17

"He delivered me from my strong enemy, and from them which hated me: for they were too strong for me. They prevented me in the day of my calamity: but the LORD was my stay. He brought me forth also into a large place; he delivered me, because he delighted in me."

Psalm 18:17-19

"And he said unto them, I beheld Satan as lightning fall from heaven. Behold, I give unto you power to tread on serpents and scorpions, and over all the power of the enemy: and nothing shall by any

means hurt you. Notwithstanding in this rejoice not, that the spirits are subject unto you; but rather rejoice, because your names are written in heaven."

Luke 10:18-20

"The LORD shall cause thine enemies that rise up against thee to be smitten before thy face: they shall come out against thee one way, and flee before thee seven ways."

Deuteronomy 28:7

"Therefore all they that devour thee shall be devoured; and all thine adversaries, every one of them, shall go into captivity; and they that spoil thee shall be a spoil, and all that prey upon thee will I give for a prey. For I will restore health unto thee, and I will heal thee of thy wounds, saith the LORD; because they called thee an Outcast, saying, This is Zion, whom no man seeketh after."

Jeremiah 30:16-17

DAY 14
The Windows of Heaven are Open

"And he saith unto him, Verily, verily, I say unto you, Hereafter ye shall see heaven open, and the angels of God ascending and descending upon the Son of man."

John 1:51

The miracles of God are not for sale, no matter how many radio or television evangelists try to sell you a "miracle cloth" or "miracle water." It's actually kind of amazing how anything can sound spiritual if you put the word "miracle" in front of it, like "miracle plant" or "miracle oil." But, the Spirit of God is not for sale. Just look at how vehemently Peter responded to Simon when he suggested that he might purchase the power to lay hands on people and have them receive the Holy Spirit.

"And when Simon saw that through laying on of the apostles' hands the Holy Ghost was given, he offered them money, Saying, Give me also this power, that on whomsoever I lay hands, he may receive the Holy Ghost. But Peter said unto him, Thy money perish with thee, because thou hast thought that the gift

of God may be purchased with money. Thou hast neither part nor lot in this matter: for thy heart is not right in the sight of God. Repent therefore of this thy wickedness, and pray God, if perhaps the thought of thine heart may be forgiven thee. For I perceive that thou art in the gall of bitterness, and in the bond of iniquity."

Acts 8:18-23

Although money is not the answer to your miracle, it would be a huge mistake not to discuss the importance of being in covenant with God. We come into covenant with God through faith. Faith is the foundation of our covenant with God. In the Old Testament, a covenant was usually sealed with blood. However, because the redemptive blood of Jesus Christ was shed at Calvary as the supreme and eternal sacrifice, faith is now the foundation of our covenant with God. We are not only in a faith covenant with the Lord for the salvation of our eternal soul, but we are also in covenant with God for our sustenance.

Tithing, for the most part, is over-taught and under-practiced in our churches. The word "tithe" literally means *"one-tenth."* I believe the Word of God clearly teaches the first tenth of your gross income, along with an offering, belongs to God (Malachi 3:10-12). I read a few statistics about giving in evangelical churches and less than six percent of members honestly tithe.

There are so many wonderful blessings promised to the person who comes into a tithing covenant with the Lord. You will be blessed.

> *"And all these blessings shall come on thee, and overtake thee, if thou shalt hearken unto the voice of the LORD thy God. Blessed shalt thou be in the city, and blessed shalt thou be in the field. Blessed shall be the fruit of thy body, and the fruit of thy ground, and the fruit of thy cattle, the increase of thy kine, and the flocks of thy sheep. Blessed shall be thy basket and thy store. Blessed shalt thou be when thou comest in, and blessed shalt thou be when thou goest out."*

> **Deuteronomy 28:2-6**

Not to mention the blessings of being different than the materialism of the world through tithes and charitable giving. When you offer God the first-fruits of all that you receive, you defeat the selfish spirit of this present-day world. "Me-ism" mixed with some materialism is the most common illness of the modern Church. The tithe declares in word and deed that everything I have is not mine but His. Even I am God's property.

"Me-ism" mixed with some materialism is the most common illness of the modern Church.

One-tenth is a picture of the whole amount. The tithe on $150.00 is $15.00. The one and the five are a picture of the whole amount of one hundred and fifty. In this way, the tithe is a type and shadow of the whole. God is interested in blessing the whole amount. That is one reason why the Lord has chosen a tenth because of its powerful symbolism of the whole. No other percentage, such as seven percent or twenty percent would have these amazing properties. Many church members are guilty of filling out their giving envelopes and marking it as tithe; however, if it is not a tenth, then it is not a tithe. The tenth is our way of saying to God that all that we have belongs to Him; the tenth is God's way of saying, "I will bless the whole."

Have you ever had seasons in your walk with God when you felt like you couldn't get a prayer through no matter what you tried? I have. It's frustrating to feel like your prayers are bouncing back off the ceiling. You may not have realized it at the time but those feelings of frustration may have been rooted in an underlying spiritual condition. The Bible talks about when the heavens are as iron and the earth is brass.

"And I will break the pride of your power; and I will make your heaven as iron, and your earth as brass:"

Leviticus 26:19

You need an open window in the Spirit. There is an interesting thing about the windows of heaven. It can be closed over your head and wide open over the person standing next to you. The Bible tells us of two men in a field:

> *"Two men shall be in the field; the one shall be taken, and the other left."*

> Luke 17:36

One of them had an open window and the other one was left behind. But, in Malachi, it tells us of one way we can insure the windows of heaven are open over our life.

> *"Bring ye all the tithes into the storehouse, that there may be meat in mine house, and prove me now herewith, saith the LORD of hosts, if I will not open you the windows of heaven, and pour you out a blessing, that there shall not be room enough to receive it."*

> **Malachi 3:10**

This covenant promise to tithers is extremely important, especially if you are trying to get a prayer through.

When you offer God your tithes and offerings, it is a form of worship. Our offering serves to honor and remember Christ. Tithing is our firstfruit offering and Christ is the firstfruit of the resurrection.

> *"But now is Christ risen from the dead, and become the firstfruits of them that slept."*

> **1 Corinthians 15:20**

This form of worship honors Christ and opens up the heavens for the favor and blessing of the Lord. If you are not presently living under an open window, then I encourage you to come into covenant with God through your tithes and offerings. When you are in a covenant, your battles become the battles of your covenant partner. If you are already a faithful tither, then take hold of your covenant promise and know that the Lord will rebuke the devourer for your sake.

> **"And I will rebuke the devourer for your sakes, and he shall not destroy the fruits of your ground; neither shall your vine cast her fruit before the time in the field, saith the LORD of hosts."**
>
> **Malachi 3:11**

Even the angel of the Lord confronted the forces of darkness with the phrase, *". . . The Lord rebuke thee!"*

> **"Yet Michael the archangel, when contending with the devil he disputed about the body of Moses, durst not bring against him a railing accusation, but said, The Lord rebuke thee."**
>
> **Jude 1:9**

You have entered into an alliance with the armies of heaven and the Lord Himself will rebuke the devil out of your situation. Jesus lived His entire earthly life under this open heaven and described it in John 1:51 saying, *". . . hereafter you shall see angels ascending and descending upon the Son of Man."* Offer God the complete ownership of everything you have—including you, your past, present, and your future. When the windows of heaven are open to you, then you will see the manifestation of God's power in your life.

Scripture Meditations

"Then Elisha said, Hear ye the word of the LORD; Thus saith the LORD, To morrow about this time shall a measure of fine flour be sold for a shekel, and two measures of barley for a shekel, in the gate of Samaria. Then a lord on whose hand the king leaned answered the man of God, and said, Behold, if the LORD would make windows in heaven, might this thing be? And he said, Behold, thou shalt see it with thine eyes, but shalt not eat thereof. And there were four leprous men at the entering in of the gate: and they said one to another, Why sit we here until we die? If we say, We will enter into the city, then the famine is in the city, and we shall die there: and if we sit still here, we die also. Now therefore come, and let us fall unto the host of the Syrians: if they save us alive, we shall live; and if they kill us, we shall but die. And they rose up in the twilight, to go unto the camp of the Syrians: and when they were come to the uttermost part of the camp of Syria, behold, there was no man there. For the LORD had made the host of the Syrians to hear a noise of chariots, and a noise of horses, even the noise of a great host: and they said one to another, Lo, the king of Israel hath hired against us the kings of the Hittites, and the kings of the Egyptians, to come upon us. Wherefore they arose and fled in the twilight, and left their tents, and their horses, and their asses, even the camp as it was, and fled for their life. And when these lepers came to the uttermost part of the camp, they went into one tent, and did eat and drink, and carried thence silver, and gold, and raiment, and went and hid it; and came again, and entered into another tent, and carried thence also, and went and hid it. Then they said one to another, We do not well: this day is a day of good tidings, and we hold our peace: if we tarry till the morning light, some mischief will come upon us: now therefore come, that we may go and tell the king's household. So they came and called unto the porter of the city: and they told them, saying, We came to the camp of the Syrians, and, behold, there was no man there, neither voice of man, but horses tied, and asses tied, and the tents as they were. And he called the porters; and they told it to the king's house within. And the king arose in the night, and said unto his servants, I will now shew you what the Syrians have done to us. They know that we be hungry; therefore are they gone out of the camp to hide themselves in the field, saying, When they come out of the city, we shall catch them alive, and get into the city. And one of his servants answered and said, Let some take, I pray thee, five of the horses that remain, which are left in the city, (behold, they are as all the multitude of Israel that are left in it: behold, I say, they are even as all the multitude of the Israelites that are consumed:) and let us send and see. They took therefore two chariot horses; and the king sent after the host of the Syrians, saying, Go and see. And they went after them unto Jordan: and, lo, all the way was full of garments and vessels, which the Syrians had cast away in their haste. And the messengers returned, and told the king. And the people went out, and spoiled the tents of the Syrians. So a measure of fine flour was sold for a shekel, and two measures of barley for a shekel, according to the word of the LORD. And the king appointed the lord on whose hand he leaned to have the charge of the gate: and the people trode upon him in the gate, and he died, as the man of God had said, who spake when the king came down to him. And it came to pass as the man of God had spoken to the king, saying, Two measures of barley for a shekel, and a measure of fine flour for a shekel, shall be to morrow about this time in the gate of Samaria: And that lord answered the man of God, and said, Now, behold, if the LORD should make windows in heaven, might such a thing be? And he said, Behold, thou shalt see it with thine eyes, but shalt not eat thereof."

2 Kings 7:1-19

"It is not expedient for me doubtless to glory. I will come to visions and revelations of the Lord. I knew a man in Christ above fourteen years ago, (whether in the body, I cannot tell; or whether out of the body, I cannot tell: God knoweth;) such an one caught up to the third heaven. And I knew such a man, (whether in the body, or out of the body, I cannot tell: God knoweth;) How that he was caught up into paradise, and heard unspeakable words, which it is not lawful for a man to utter."

2 Corinthians 12:1-4

"After this I looked, and, behold, a door was opened in heaven: and the first voice which I heard was as it were of a trumpet talking with me; which said, Come up hither, and I will shew thee *things which must be hereafter. And immediately I was in the spirit: and, behold, a throne was set in heaven, and one sat on the throne."*

Revelation 4:1-2

Day 15
Help Thou My Unbelief

"And let us not be weary in well doing:
for in due season we shall reap,
if we faint not."

Galatians 6:9

Faith is that incredible, intangible force that allows us to build a bridge upon which God's miracle power can cross. It is unique in that it is a fruit of the Spirit, as well as a gift of the Spirit. This tells us something very important about acquiring the faith for a miracle. Since it is a fruit of the Spirit, it can be cultivated and grown. Now, I realize we are no longer an agricultural society. As a matter of fact, we are more of a microwave society. We want it now. *"Hello, I'm waiting!"* Most of us are used to talking into the clown's mouth and out pops a cheeseburger. I once saw a commercial for a product called the "Salad Shooter.®" Since people can no longer wait for the vegetables to be picked up off the cutting board, the Salad Shooter® propels them right into the bowl. Grandma never had one of those back on the farm.

There is nothing wrong with our pace of life as long as our priorities remain steadfast. Our fast-paced life does make it increasingly difficult to relate to the patient farmer who faithfully watches over his crop through the long, hot summer. We may also have difficulty understanding the concept of a controlled environment. This is a little more than raising the thermostat on a cold, winter night. You must consider the best possible climate, soil, moisture, exposure to the sun, nutrients, and a host other environmental influences. Yet, none of this—even if done perfectly—will guarantee growth; but it will definitely make good growth more probable. Just like a greenhouse which allows plants to grow in the best possible temperature and humidity, your faith will increase in a controlled environment. Your faith cannot be manufactured, but it can be cultivated.

If you will make a conscious effort to provide the best possible atmosphere for your faith to grow, the fruit of the Spirit, faith, will begin to blossom.

Your faith cannot be manufactured; it must be cultivated.

The next question is, "What spiritual climate will allow my faith to grow?" Well, let's examine the basics of spiritual agronomy.[1] A healthy plant needs soil, sun, water, and the appropriate temperature. I believe that there is a strong spiritual parallel for each of these natural requirements for plant growth. First, you are the soil.

"And the LORD God formed man of the dust of the ground, and breathed into his nostrils the breath of life; and man became a living soul."

Genesis 2:7

Second, the sun is symbolized by the presence of God.

"And the city had no need of the sun, neither of the moon, to shine in it: for the glory of God did lighten it, and the Lamb is the light thereof."

Revelations 21:23

"Who coverest thyself with light as with a garment: who stretchest out the heavens like a curtain:"

Psalm 104:2

The presence of God is presently manifested through the Holy Spirit.

"Nevertheless I tell you the truth; It is expedient for you that I go away: for if I go not away, the Comforter will not come unto you; but if I depart, I will send him unto you."

John 16:7

Third, the water is the Word of God.

"That he might sanctify and cleanse it with the washing of water by the word,"

Ephesians 5:26

This is also made clear when the Bible says in Romans 10:17, *"So then faith cometh by hearing, and hearing by the word of God."*

In any garden, weeds are definitely factors in the growth of healthy plants. Weeds can constrict growth and rob plants of much-needed nutrients and moisture. In providing your faith a proper environment for maximum growth, careful consideration must be given for potential weeds. An Old Testament verse may give insight to what may be a potential "weed" capable of choking the life out of your faith.

"I create the fruit of the lips; Peace, peace to him that is far off, and to him that is near, saith the LORD; and I will heal him."

Isaiah 57:19

It makes a great deal of sense that if you can sow fruit with good words then you can certainly sow weeds as well. Perhaps the negative words which can potentially take root in our mind and spirit play the role of the weed in our faith's growth and development. It's easy to see how negative words can choke the very life out of our faith.

It never hurts to add a little spiritual "Miracle Grow®" in the form of a testimony. The power of a personal testimony can spur on the growth of your own personal faith for miracles. In the same way that negative and critical words can harm your faith, encouraging words can bring life. The Bible says in Revelation 12:11, *"And they overcame him by the blood of the Lamb, and by the word of their testimony; and they loved not their lives unto the death."*

This may be taking our metaphor a bit too far but I want to be certain you understand the benefits of reading and listening to personal testimonies of the healing power of God. This will cause your faith to grow at an incredible rate.

If careful attention is given to each facet of your spiritual climate, you will soon be enjoying the benefits of faith. Faith is the key to your miracle. This simple concept of faith-growing, rather than faith-building, can help you reach a new potential in God. Stop looking for formulas to manufacture faith, but rather cultivate your faith. Give it what it needs to grow and mature. Faith is not only a bridge to the miraculous; it is that intangible glue that allows us to hold on to the unseen hand of God even when everything in your life is shaking.

Like every farmer or gardener, there is an innate understanding of the process of seedtime and harvest. It's not something a lawyer can articulate in a contract. It's not the kind of thing one could ever take for granted. It's really hard to put into words which neither underestimate nor exaggerate the principle, so I'll try to boil it down to its simplest form: if you do what you can do, then God will do what only He can do.

"So then neither is he that planteth any thing, neither he that watereth; but God that giveth the increase."

1 Corinthians 3:7

Only God can make a tree. All of our efforts must be overshadowed by the fact that only God can breathe life into a seed.

Your desire for an ever-growing and increasing faith should not be wholly motivated by your need, but rather by your desire to know God and trust Him. It's not faith *alone*; it is faith *in God* alone. Harvest the faith in your heart to see God as you never have before. Faith is like the pair of spectacles or binoculars which allows you to see what is already there with more clarity. Abraham was often called the father of faith

> **"Your father Abraham rejoiced to see my day: and he saw it, and was glad."**
>
> **John 8:56**

Make your home a greenhouse for your faith. Let it be a house of prayer. Always have a Bible at arm's length. Let anointed songs and sermons feed your spirit night and day. Fellowship with people who lift your faith and share testimonies of what the Lord has done. Tell those critical and negative weeds in your life to SHUT UP in Jesus name!

> **"Neither give place to the devil."**
>
> **Ephesians 4:27**

Finally, be patient like the old farmer. Sometimes you can't see it day to day; but come fall, it's harvest time.

Scripture Meditations

"But the fruit of the Spirit is love, joy, peace, long-suffering, gentleness, goodness, faith, meekness, temperance: against such there is no law."

Galatians 5:22-23

"While the earth remaineth, seedtime and harvest, and cold and heat, and summer and winter, and day and night shall not cease."

Genesis 8:22

"I am the true vine, and my Father is the husbandman. Every branch in me that beareth not fruit he taketh away: and every branch that beareth fruit, he purgeth it, that it may bring forth more fruit. Now ye are clean through the word which I have spoken unto you. Abide in me, and I in you. As the branch cannot bear fruit of itself, except it abide in the vine; no more can ye, except ye abide in me. I am the vine, ye are the branches: He that abideth in me, and I in him, the same bringeth forth much fruit: for without me ye can do nothing. If a man abide not in me, he is cast forth as a branch, and is withered; and men gather them, and cast them into the fire, and they are burned. If ye abide in me, and my words abide in you, ye shall ask what ye will, and it shall be done unto you. Herein is my Father

glorified, that ye bear much fruit; so shall ye be my disciples."

John 15:1-8

"Not boasting of things without our measure, that is, of other men's labours; but having hope, when your faith is increased, that we shall be enlarged by you according to our rule abundantly,"

2 Corinthians 10:15

"For night and day we pray on and on for you, asking God to let us see you again, to fill up any little cracks there may yet be in your faith."

1 Thessalonians 3:9-10 (TLB)

"But grow in grace, and in the knowledge of our Lord and Saviour Jesus Christ. To him be glory both now and for ever. Amen."

2 Peter 3:18

"I have planted, Apollos watered; but God gave the increase. So then neither is he that planteth any thing, neither he that watereth; but God that giveth the increase."

1 Corinthians 3:6-7

"And the Lord make you to increase and abound in love one toward another, and toward all men, even as we do toward you:"

1 Thessalonians 3:12

"Blessed is the man that walketh not in the counsel of the ungodly, nor standeth in the way of sinners, nor sitteth in the seat of the scornful. But his delight is in the law of the LORD; and in his law doth he meditate day and night. And he shall be like a tree planted by the rivers of water, that bringeth forth his fruit in his season; his leaf also shall not wither; and whatsoever he doeth shall prosper."

Psalm 1:1-3

"Then I will give you rain in due season, and the land shall yield her increase, and the trees of the field shall yield their fruit."

Leviticus 26:4

Day 16

Take Action

"For as the body without the spirit is dead, so faith without works is dead also."

James 2:26

You must do something to put your faith to work. Faith requires activation. Have you ever wondered why so often in Scripture God required some form of action before He would move? Why ask a man as influential and important as Naaman to dip seven times in the muddy river Jordan?[1] Or, have you ever wondered what was up with the clay and spittle when Jesus healed the blind man?[2] It seems that upon reflection, the Lord is in the habit of requiring something of us when He does the miraculous.

There are some who might say at this point, "Jesus paid it all." I would have to agree with that statement, but doesn't it make a whole lot of sense that if we truly believe Jesus paid it all, then we would act accordingly? Doesn't faith require us to act as if it has already happened? Doesn't this confidence in Christ's full payment call for a response?

"Now faith is the substance of things hoped for, the evidence of things not seen."

Hebrews 11:1

If faith is the substance, then what is it? Where is it? Can I touch it? "Substance" means "that which is solid and practical in character, quality, or importance."[3] Your actions substantiate your beliefs. What is this "evidence of things not seen"? I believe it is the actions and attitudes of someone who is thoroughly convinced of something. For instance, if you are convinced it is going to rain, then you might roll up your car windows or carry an umbrella. Each of these actions would be a tangible witness of your belief that it will surely rain, although no one has seen a drop yet. Someone might think you look silly with a raincoat on, but that wouldn't bother you at all if you were completely convinced.

Let's imagine what it must have been like to be blind in the first century. There were no schools to help you function in society. There were no government checks for your disability. There were no books written in Braille. Most had no choice but to beg for a living. Can you picture the dust and animal dung that must have lined the streets of Jerusalem? And there along the roadside, wearing the beggar's garment, was a man blind from birth. Jesus heard his cry and mixed clay and spittle together and covered his eyes with the concoction. Then, He instructed the blind man to go wash his dirt-covered eyes in the pool of Siloam.

Many years ago, we went on a tour of Squire Boone Caverns in Indiana. One of the friends who came with us was blind. When we were deep inside the cave, the tour guide said he was going to show us something that most of us had probably never seen before. Because of sunlight, moonlight, and starlight, as well as all the artificial sources of light today, it's a truly rare place that one can experience absolute darkness. So with quite a fanfare on the five-dollar tour, the guide said, "Here it is." He then switched off the lights and, in a moment, you could not see your hand in front of your face. There were no shadows or shades. Total darkness enveloped us deep inside this cave. Our blind friend blurted out, "Well, where is it!" Nothing changed for him. He lived in this place of total darkness. For a sighted person to ask a blind person to go on a scavenger hunt for their miracle seems just a little sadistic.

The blind man might have responded to Jesus by saying something like, "Hey, I'm blind, in case you haven't noticed." What would cause the blind man to simply obey and head for the pool to wash his eyes? He must have been convinced it would work. There was no healing ingredient in the pool. This was not a prescription for medicine; it was a call to action.

Your miracle is only one step of faith away.

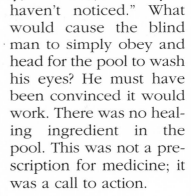

"Take up your bed and walk," is what Jesus told the lame man at the Pool of Bethesda and He is still giving out that same command of faith today (John 5:5-9). Your miracle is only one step of faith away.

The Bible says Moses had faith to take up the serpent (Numbers 21:8-9). Now, if there ever was a Biblical example which has been abused and misused, we have found one here. Many years ago in Phelps, Kentucky, I sat and listened to first-hand accounts of "snake-handling" churches. Phelps is on the West Virginia border near Matewan and Red Jacket, Kentucky. These towns are famous for the generational feud between the Hatfields and McCoys. These two families fought so long, the real reason for the start of the feud was forgotten but the hatred and fighting continued. (This is not very relevant to the topic of healing, but it definitely helps us better understand the "Appalachian Mentality" which gave rise to the ridiculous belief that the Lord wants us to pick up and handle snakes.) Many agree that is preposterous. The problem is that this crazy practice has caused me, and every other Pentecostal preacher, to just leave that verse alone. I wonder if the whole satanic plot behind snake handling isn't to keep us away from the revelation and truth in this story.

Moses had faith to obey God despite natural fear. Fear of snakes is definitely a natural fear. I have seen grown men come high steppin' out the brush like a Heisman trophy winner because they thought they saw a snake. Don't get me wrong. I'm not saying everyone is afraid of snakes—just the normal people. After all, didn't God Himself promise in the Garden that snakes would be the natural enemy of Mankind?

> **"And the LORD God said unto the serpent, Because thou hast done this, thou art cursed above all cattle, and above every beast of the field; upon thy belly shalt thou go, and dust shalt thou eat all the days of thy life: And I will put enmity between thee and the woman, and between thy seed and her seed; it shall bruise thy head, and thou shalt bruise his heel."**

> **Genesis 3:14-15**

Despite this, Moses had faith to do something unnatural which could potentially have caused him pain, even death. His faith is what brought deliverance to the nation of Israel. This doesn't mean we should each try something that could potentially kill us. That would be ridiculous. But, we should each be quick to obey the directions of the Holy Spirit regardless of natural fear.

Sometimes a step of faith is quite a stretch and yet, other times, it is something simple like when Naaman was told to dip in the Jordan River seven times. This was probably a very humbling experience for someone in Naaman's austere position in the military. Pride can be a real barrier to your blessing. At first, Naaman was upset he was asked to do something as common as bathe in the river. This is where the peasants bathed and washed their clothes. A man of means need not sully himself in the muddy Jordan, but simply have servants draw a warm bath with rare and precious ointments and perfumes. But Namaan's servant convinced him it was in his best interest to do whatever it would take. I hear in the undertone of the servant the realization of Namaan's true condition. "Yes, you are a mighty man of valor and stature who has offered great gifts for the favor of the prophet, but you are a leper. And, you are going to die like all the other lepers. Except the Lord help thee, Naaman, there is no help for you." Would you rather be dignified and dead or a muddy miracle?

The act is more than just washing in the Jordan; it's the revelation that God is our only true source of help and healing. This is a tough sell in our society today. Modern medicine puts on quite a light show, but beneath the lasers, scalpels, and pharmaceuticals is the underlining belief in the healing properties that God created in the human body. God is the source of all healing, whether it is ancient or modern or natural or supernatural. To truly believe this is to anxiously await His instruction, no matter how humbling or even seemingly unnatural. In looking at Naaman's example, it's quite possible that your miracle is beneath you. You need only bow down to receive it. Sometimes a step of faith is more than just the activation of your faith; it is a step over a boundary that is keeping you from receiving from the Lord.

One story that really inspires my faith is the story of the blind man, Bartimaeus. The Bible mentions him laying aside his garment as he comes before the Lord. This takes on a whole new meaning when you realize what the significance of the garment was back then. The blind are extremely vulnerable and oftentimes, in today's society, they will carry a white cane. This is beneficial in tapping before them, giving them warning if an object is in the way. But have you ever wondered why the cane is a highly-visible white? The reason: this helps us see the blind and identify them; and hopefully, in a caring society, watch out for them. Well, in Biblical times, a person who was blind marked themselves with a specific garment. When the blind man approached Jesus he basically threw aside his white "cane"—his garment—and stood before Jesus. Now that is an act of faith. He was basically saying, "Well, I won't need this anymore because Jesus is calling me."

Jesus paid it all, but that revelation is calling for a response from those who truly believe it. Take a step of faith today and do something that you could not do before. Do something that symbolizes and crystallizes your confidence that Jesus is calling you before Him today. If the Lord says, "Seven," six just won't do. The highest order of worship is the simple act of obedience.

Scripture Meditations

"And Moses answered and said, But, behold, they will not believe me, nor hearken unto my voice: for they will say, The LORD hath not appeared unto thee. And the LORD said unto him, What is that in thine hand? And he said, A rod. And he said, Cast it on the ground. And he cast it on the ground, and it became a serpent; and Moses fled from before it. And the LORD said unto Moses, Put forth thine hand, and take it by the tail. And he put forth his hand, and caught it, and it became a rod in his hand:"

Exodus 4:1-4

"Now Naaman, captain of the host of the king of Syria, was a great man with his master, and honourable, because by him the LORD had given deliverance unto Syria: he was also a mighty man in valour, but he was a leper. And the Syrians had gone out by companies, and had brought away captive out of the land of Israel a little maid; and she waited on Naaman's wife. And she said unto her mistress, Would God my lord were with the prophet that is in Samaria! for he would recover him of his leprosy. And one went in, and told his lord, saying, Thus and thus said the maid that is of the land of Israel. And the king of Syria said, Go to, go, and I will send a letter unto the king of Israel. And he departed, and took with him ten talents of silver, and six thousand pieces of gold,

and ten changes of raiment. And he brought the letter to the king of Israel, saying, Now when this letter is come unto thee, behold, I have therewith sent Naaman my servant to thee, that thou mayest recover him of his leprosy. And it came to pass, when the king of Israel had read the letter, that he rent his clothes, and said, Am I God, to kill and to make alive, that this man doth send unto me to recover a man of his leprosy? Wherefore consider, I pray you, and see how he seeketh a quarrel against me. And it was so, when Elisha the man of God had heard that the king of Israel had rent his clothes, that he sent to the king, saying, Wherefore hast thou rent thy clothes? Let him come now to me, and he shall know that there is a prophet in Israel. So Naaman came with his horses and with his chariot, and stood at the door of the house of Elisha. And Elisha sent a messenger unto him, saying, Go and wash in Jordan seven times, and thy flesh shall come again to thee, and thou shalt be clean. But Naaman was wroth, and went away, and said, Behold, I thought, He will surely come out to me, and stand, and call on the name of the LORD his God, and strike his hand over the place, and recover the leper. Are not Abana and Pharpar, rivers of Damascus, better than all the waters of Israel? May I not wash in them, and be clean? So he turned and went away in a rage. And his servants came near, and spake unto him, and said, My father, if the prophet had bid thee do some great thing, wouldest thou not have done it? how much rather then, when he saith to thee, Wash, and be clean? Then went he down, and dipped himself seven times in Jordan, according to the saying of the man of God: and his flesh came again like unto the flesh of a little child, and he was clean."

2 Kings 5:1-14

"And the men of the city said unto Elisha, Behold, I pray thee, the situation of this city is pleasant, as my lord seeth: but the water is naught, and the ground barren. And he said, Bring me a new cruse, and put salt therein. And they brought it to him. And he went forth unto the spring of the waters, and cast the salt in there, and said, Thus saith the LORD, I have healed these waters; there shall not be from thence any more death or barren land. So the waters were healed unto this day, according to the saying of Elisha which he spake."

2 Kings 2:19-22

"And they came to Jericho: and as he went out of Jericho with his disciples and a great number of people, blind Bartimaeus, the son of Timaeus, sat by the highway side begging. And when he heard that it was Jesus of Nazareth, he began to cry out, and say, Jesus, thou Son of David, have mercy on me. And many charged him that he should hold his peace: but he cried the more a great deal, Thou Son of David, have mercy on me. And Jesus stood still, and commanded him to be called. And they call the blind man, saying unto him, Be of good comfort, rise; he calleth thee. And he, casting away his garment, rose, and came to Jesus. And Jesus answered and said unto him, What wilt thou that I should do unto thee? The blind man said unto him, Lord, that I might receive my sight. And Jesus said unto him, Go thy way; thy faith hath made thee whole. And immediately he received his sight, and followed Jesus in the way."

Mark 10:46-52

"But that ye may know that the Son of man hath power on earth to forgive sins, (then saith he to the sick of the palsy,) Arise, take up thy bed, and go unto thine house."

Matthew 9:6

"And as Jesus passed by, he saw a man which was blind from his birth. And his disciples asked him, saying, Master, who did sin, this man, or his parents, that he was born blind? Jesus answered, Neither hath this man sinned, nor his parents: but that the works of God should be made manifest in him. I must work the works of him that sent me, while it is day: the night cometh, when no man can work. As long as I am in the world, I am the light of the world. When he had thus spoken, he spat on the ground, and made clay of the spittle, and he anointed the eyes of the blind man with the clay, And said unto him, Go, wash in the pool of Siloam, (which is by interpretation, Sent.) He went his way therefore, and washed, and came seeing. The neighbours therefore, and they which before had seen him that he was blind, said, Is not this he that sat and begged?"

John 9:1-8

Day 17

Healing in the Old Testament

> "O LORD my God, I cried unto thee, and thou
> hast healed me."
>
> Psalm 30:2

Does the Lord really concern Himself with our bodies? After all, isn't He really just looking at our spirit and soul? You may be surprised to discover just how much the Lord has shown His care and concern for the health of His people. From the perfect physical health of Adam and Eve before the Fall to the miracles of the Apostles, we see God has a special interest in our physical condition. There were at least two and one-half million people in the mass exodus from Egypt and the Bible says, *"He brought them forth also with silver and gold: and there was not one feeble person among their tribes,"* (Psalm 105:37).[1]

Caleb is a fascinating example in the Old Testament of the Lord blessing someone with divine health.

"And now, behold, the LORD hath kept me alive, as he said, these forty and five years, even since the LORD spake this word unto Moses, while the children of Israel wandered

in the wilderness: and now, lo, I am this day fourscore and five years old. As yet I am as strong this day as I was in the day that Moses sent me: as my strength was then, even so is my strength now, for war, both to go out, and to come in."

Joshua 14:10-11

Caleb was over eighty years old but was as strong as he was in his forties. Everyone over fifty knows that is miracle! The Old Testament is full of examples of God's healing nature.

"And Moses was an hundred and twenty years old when he died: his eye was not dim, nor his natural force abated."

Deuteronomy 34:7

Moses is another example of divine health. You must realize that healing is not a New Testament metaphor for "forgiveness." Healing is not limited to the lifetime of Jesus and the Apostles; healing is, and always has been, the nature of God. When Hezekiah was "sick unto death," he cried to the Lord and the Lord healed him and added fifteen years to his life (2 Kings 20:1-11).

Healing is not limited to the life-time of Jesus and the Apostles; healing is, and always has been, the nature of God.

Naaman was a decorated soldier, but he was also a leper. A servant mentioned to him the fact that there was a prophet in Israel who could do something about his leprosy. That assumption speaks volumes about how the Israelites felt and believed God could and would heal. Naaman's king sent a letter of introduction to the King of Israel referencing Naaman's condition. As the story goes, the miracle takes place in the Jordan River as Naaman follows the prophet's prescription.

Another example is the story of the Shunammite woman who was healed of barrenness.

"And he said, What then is to be done for her? And Gehazi answered, Verily she hath no child, and her husband is old. And he said, Call her. And when he had called her, she stood in the door. And he said, About this season, according to the time of life, thou shalt embrace a son. And she said, Nay, my lord, thou man of God, do not lie unto thine handmaid. And the woman conceived, and bare a son at that season that Elisha had said unto her, according to the time of life."

2 Kings 4:14-17

Then later, her son was raised from the dead after a sunstroke. Rebekah was healed of barrenness after Isaac prayed to God.

"And Isaac intreated the LORD for his wife, because she was barren: and the LORD was intreated of him, and Rebekah his wife conceived."

Genesis 25:21

God took pity upon Leah and opened up her womb.

> **"And when the LORD saw that Leah was hated, he opened her womb: but Rachel was barren."**

> **Genesis 29:31**

A less famous Old Testament man was named Manoah. His wife could not have children.

> **"And there was a certain man of Zorah, of the family of the Danites, whose name was Manoah; and his wife was barren, and bare not. And the angel of the LORD appeared unto the woman, and said unto her, Behold now, thou art barren, and bearest not: but thou shalt conceive, and bear a son."**

> **Judges 13:2-3**

That son grew up to be none other than the mighty Samson. With Israel's rich history of God healing the impotent and barren, David sings of God's healing nature.

> **"He maketh the barren woman to keep house, and to be a joyful mother of children. Praise ye the LORD."**

> **Psalm 113:9**

The Lord included in the laws and rituals of the covenant certain ceremonies that could confirm His miracles.

> **"And the priest shall go forth out of the camp; and the priest shall look, and, behold, if the plague of leprosy be healed in the leper;"**

Leviticus 14:3

There is no cure for leprosy—even today—so this ritual was only necessary because of the Lord's propensity to heal.

Many of the rituals of the Hebrew covenant were the Lord's protection of His children. Many nations were completely wiped out by eating improperly preserved and prepared foods. Trichinosis and many other diseases plagued humanity because of the lack of knowledge and understanding of bacteria and micro-organisms. Much of modern medicine's understanding of sanitation and the spread of disease has only served to give credence to the laws of God.

When Peter had his vision of the table and was released to eat and enjoy things previously thought unclean by the Jews, it correlated with a time in human history when the understanding of food preparation, particularly meat, had removed most danger from what was previously non-kosher.[2] This, again, reveals the Lord's concern over His children's physical condition.

The Lord had Moses erect a pole with a brazen serpent so that the people could be healed of snakebites (Numbers 21:9). This remains the symbol of healing and medicine to this day.

Scripture Meditations

"So Abraham prayed unto God: and God healed Abimelech, and his wife, and his maidservants; and they bare children."

Genesis 20:17

"And said, If thou wilt diligently hearken to the voice of the LORD thy God, and wilt do that which is right in his sight, and wilt give ear to his commandments, and keep all his statutes, I will put none of these diseases upon thee, which I have brought upon the Egyptians: for I am the LORD that healeth thee."

Exodus 15:26

"Who forgiveth all thine iniquities; who healeth all thy diseases;"

Psalm 103:3

"He healeth the broken in heart, and bindeth up their wounds."

Psalm 147:3

"Moreover the light of the moon shall be as the light of the sun, and the light of the sun shall be sevenfold, as the light of seven days, in the day that the LORD bindeth up the breach of his people, and healeth the stroke of their wound."

Isaiah 30:26

"He sent his word, and healed them, and delivered them from their destructions."

Psalm 107:20

"Christ hath redeemed us from the curse of the law,
being made a curse for us: . . ."

Galatians 3:13

Is it possible to live in divine health? Is it an
expectation beyond the promises of Scripture to
believe and hope for continued health? Isn't it
enough that the Lord has made provisions for our
healing through the cross? In today's world of
supplements and exercise it really is the topic of the
day: "How do I get and stay healthy?" It is interesting
to note that Christ was never sick. He was wounded,
of course, but there is not a single reference to Christ
being sick. Hmmm?

**"In the beginning God created the heavens
and the earth."**

Genesis 1:1

There are many who have fallen prey to the pseudo-
science of evolution. Evolution is the belief that a
tornado can go through a junkyard and a Swiss
watch come out on the other side. There is no
missing link. There is a missing chain! It's important

for you to realize that God created you and you were designed originally to live forever.

> *"And the LORD God commanded the man, saying, Of every tree of the garden thou mayest freely eat: But of the tree of the knowledge of good and evil, thou shalt not eat of it: for in the day that thou eatest thereof thou shalt surely die."*
>
> **Genesis 2:16-17**

Sin is the culprit. The price of sin is death. If you take sin out of the equation, Man was created to live forever. Sin is the original source of all sickness, pain, disease, and death.

Perhaps one of the most condensed truths in Scripture is this: what was lost in the first Adam is gained in the Second Adam—Jesus.

> *"For as in Adam all die, even so in Christ shall all be made alive."*
>
> **1 Corinthians 15:22**

This could germinate study after study into the terrible cost of sin to humanity and the amazing restoration of Calvary. We gained access through the Lord Jesus Christ to walk with God again in the Garden. But, if there is a restoration of relationship, then there must also be a restoration of benefits. To be free from sin is to be free from the *curse* of sin, which includes sickness. There is an opportunity for believers to walk in freedom from sin *and* sickness. How narrow-minded to believe that Christ has conquered death but not disease. The Pharisees criticized Christ for telling someone who had just received a miracle, "Thy sins be forgiven thee." They thought, "Who in the world does this man, Jesus, think he is forgiving sins?"

Jesus responds to their accusations with a rather interesting question:

"Whether is easier, to say, Thy sins be forgiven thee; or to say, Rise up and walk?"

Luke 5:23

This question leaves them stupefied and unable to respond. The real answer to the question is that it's the same.

The Old Testament records the story of several people—Moses and Caleb, to name a few—whose natural health was supernaturally sustained by God. Then, there is the incredible miracle of Abraham and Sarah having a son way past the age of child-bearing years (Genesis 21:1-7). These testimonies show that even in the Old Testament the Lord manifested His nature not only to heal, but also to give his chosen people divine health. Some might think if the curse of sin is broken, then no true Christian should ever die; but that is not what God has promised. Death is a part of the cycle of life. It is appointed unto man once to die and after this the judgment (Hebrews 9:27). None of these Old Testament examples lived forever. What Jesus did was to remove the *sting* of death. Death is simply a portal through which we pass from this life to the life which is to come. Paul said to be absent from the body is to be present with the Lord (2 Corinthians 5:8). You have a set time on this side of glory and you should not have to waste it being sick, especially when the Bible says, *"by His stripes you were healed,"* (1 Peter 2:24).

There is a story about the apostle Paul which points to a near death experience in which Paul was stoned.

> **"And there came thither certain Jews from Antioch and Iconium, who persuaded the people, and, having stoned Paul, drew him out of the city, supposing he had been dead."**
>
> **Acts 14:19**

This story shows us that as long as the purpose of God is still before you, then God will heal disease, even injury. Nero's chopping block was Paul's destiny. Prophets warned Paul long before he got to Rome, to which he responded, "I know but I've got to go." Although we have had the privilege of reading ahead and we know that Paul was destined to die in Rome, things in Iconium turned out to be quite a miracle. Paul still had things to do and a few more letters to write. And so, we see God raising him up from near death so he can continue the work of the Lord. If you know God has a call on your life in which you have yet to finish, then you need not worry about this thing that looks like it could be the end. You have every right to be healed and come up out of that pile of rocks and complete your mission.

Smith Wigglesworth believed in divine health and claimed this promise for himself despite a long battle with kidney stones. Eventually, he was healed and lived a long life without sickness or disease. A doctor who was present when Reverend Wigglesworth passed away estimated his age at twenty years younger than the Reverend's actual age. This doctor's account reminds me of the description of Moses.

"And Moses was an hundred and twenty years old when he died: his eye was not dim, nor his natural force abated."

Deuteronomy 34:7

Back in the nineteen seventies and eighties, when I was growing up in the Pentecostal church, we still had "old school" testimony services. I will never forget Sister Rosa Lee Long and how she would testify every chance she could get. She would say, "I have been saved for sixty-five years and filled with His precious Holy Ghost and I am living proof that the same God that can save, can keep you. There is a keeping power, Brother Jimmy. I haven't taken so much as an aspirin in those sixty-five years. Jesus is my aspirin. He is my healer." That seems like such a long time ago, but God hasn't changed. It just might be that we really don't expect much, and so therefore, we don't receive much.

. . . it is not God's ultimate goal to rescue you; God's nature is abundance.

Personally, I don't think it is wrong to go to the doctor or to take a pill for a headache. Nevertheless, I do think we should give God the first opportunity to move in our lives. One thing I know for sure is if we don't believe it, we will never see it. I have reached a point in my life where I don't really have time to be sick; not because of kids and work and bills and traffic, but rather, because I must be about my Father's business.

Here is a theological revelation for you: it is not God's ultimate goal to rescue you; God's nature is abundance.

"For I know the plans I have for you," declares the LORD, "plans to prosper you and not to harm you, plans to give you hope and a future."

Jeremiah 29:10-12 (NIV)

God is not the God of just enough; He is El Shaddai, the God who is more than enough. The God of superfluity. The God of a cornucopia. What you need is to reach beyond "just enough faith to pull through," to a vision of yourself completely whole. There is definitely a difference between being *healed* and being made *whole*.

In the book of Luke, there were ten lepers who were cleansed by Jesus, but only one came back to thank him. To that leper, the Bible says Jesus told him, ". . . thy faith hath made thee whole."

"And one of them, when he saw that he was healed, turned back, and with a loud voice glorified God, And fell down on his face at his feet, giving him thanks: and he was a Samaritan. And Jesus answering said, Were there not ten cleansed? but where are the nine? There are not found that returned to give glory to God, save this stranger. And he

said unto him, Arise, go thy way: thy faith hath made thee whole."

Luke 17:15-19

Our expectation of Jesus should not be just healing but to be made whole. "Whole" means that nothing is missing. The leprosy may have caused the loss of fingers and toes, but Jesus made the man whole. Beyond the faith for a miracle is the faith to be made whole and to live in divine health so that you might accomplish the purposes of God.

You are fearfully and wonderfully made (Psalm 139:14). You don't have to give in to sickness, injury, or even old age.

"But if the Spirit of him that raised up Jesus from the dead dwell in you, he that raised up Christ from the dead shall also quicken your mortal bodies by his Spirit that dwelleth in you."

Romans 8:11

"Quicken" means *"to cause to live to make alive."* If you have the faith to walk in divine health, then our God has the propensity and the power.

Scripture Meditations

"And Asa in the thirty and ninth year of his reign was diseased in his feet, until his disease was exceeding great: yet in his disease he sought not to the LORD, but to the physicians. And Asa slept with his fathers, and died in the one and fortieth year of his reign."

2 Chronicles 16:12-13

"A Psalm of David. Bless the LORD, O my soul: and all that is within me, bless his holy name. Bless the LORD, O my soul, and forget not all his benefits: Who forgiveth all thine iniquities; who healeth all thy diseases; Who redeemeth thy life from destruction; who crowneth thee with lovingkindness and tender mercies;"

Psalm 103:1-4

"And the very God of peace sanctify you wholly; and I pray God your whole spirit and soul and body be preserved blameless unto the coming of our Lord Jesus Christ. Faithful is he that calleth you, who also will do it."

1 Thessalonians 5:23-24

"O death, where is thy sting? O grave, where is thy victory? The sting of death is sin; and the strength of sin is the law. But thanks be to God, which giveth us the victory through our Lord Jesus Christ."

1 Corinthians 15:55-57

"My son, attend to my words; incline thine ear unto my sayings. Let them not depart from thine eyes; keep them in the midst of thine heart. For they are life unto those that find them, and health to all their flesh. Keep thy heart with all diligence; for out of it are the issues of life."

Proverbs 4:20-23

"And being not weak in faith, he con-sidered not his own body now dead, when he was about an hundred years old, neither yet the deadness of Sara's womb: He staggered not at the promise of God through unbelief; but was strong in faith, giving glory to God; And being fully persuaded that, what he had promised, he was able also to perform."

Romans 4:19-21

Day 19

Strong Defense

"O LORD, my strength, and my fortress, and my
refuge in the day of affliction, . . ."

Jeremiah 16:19

Have you ever had a coach tell you the best offense is a strong defense? It's rather difficult to be defeated by a team who never scores against you. If our desire is to walk in the Spirit and accomplish the purpose of God in our life, then we should consider the importance of having a strong defense. Satan comes to steal and destroy (John 10:10). Sickness and disease are two of his greatest weapons. Sickness steals your joy, time, and productivity. We must build our defenses so the enemy cannot easily come and plunder our precious promises.

> **"Wherefore take unto you the whole armour of God, that ye may be able to withstand in the evil day, and having done all, to stand. Stand therefore, having your loins girt about with truth, and having on the breastplate of righteousness; And your feet shod with the preparation of the gospel of peace; Above all, taking the shield of faith, wherewith ye shall**

be able to quench all the fiery darts of the wicked. And take the helmet of salvation, and the sword of the Spirit, which is the word of God:"

Ephesians 6:13-17

A strong defense begins with our personal body armor. Each and every part is critical and holds important spiritual significance in our lives. Spiritual warfare is a much-abused topic; but nonetheless, we wrestle not against flesh and blood but against principalities and powers (Ephesians 6:12). The Bible does say above all to take up the shield of faith (Ephesians 6:16). This is our most important defense mechanism. Even if we are deficient in other areas, the shield of faith can cover those areas during an engagement with the enemy. In your walk with God, the passion to pursue Him through study and to experience greater faith is paramount to your spiritual defenses.

"For therein is the righteousness of God revealed from faith to faith: as it is written, the just shall live by faith."

Romans 1:17

Each victory becomes a building block for bigger battles won. Faith can quench all the fiery darts of the enemy, including spirits of affliction.

What about exercise, vitamins, supplements, and eating right? This is a hill many ministries have died on. The minute we begin to try to legislate holiness, we open ourselves up for a religious spirit. Religion and legalism are two kindred spirits which can appeal to a minister's desperate desire to protect their flock from the ravenous wolves of sin. These spirits offer rules without reason and bring people under condemnation, rather than promoting personal spiritual growth. It produces co-dependent believers incapable of being led by the Spirit. I have seen people take the Word of God and twist it to fit their stringent, vegetarian lifestyle. Yet, others take the same Bible and use to justify a super-sized big burger— everything—combo meal with a diet drink.

I want to be really careful here and not bring condemnation into your life. Perhaps, the most balanced message I've ever heard on the topic of eating right was from Pastor Louis Kayatin from Lorain, Ohio. What he said convicted, without religion. He said the reason he exercises every morning and eats right is because he has a mandate and call of God on his life and simply does not have time to be sick. When we become connected with our eternal purpose, we will lay some things down which slow us down; not because we have to, but because we want to. The Bible says in Hebrews 12:1, *". . . Let us lay aside every weight, and the sin which doth so easily beset us, . . ."* Some things are not a matter of

> When we become connected with our eternal purpose, we will lay some things down which slow us down; not because we have to, but because we want to.

sin, but rather they are a weight which slows us down.

Look at all the truly great athletes. They don't practice and train because they have to; they do it because they want to. Certain productive lifestyle changes can be a great source of protection against sickness, disease, and theft of our time and energy. This is not *instead of* believing for miracles and healing, but *in addition* to believing for miracles and healing. If you truly understand the significance of your mission in life, then you will not find it so hard to imagine the devil doing everything he can think of to slow you down. In turn, you should create every wall and barrier possible to protect yourself from satanic distractions.

> **"We know that whosoever is born of God sinneth not; but he that is begotten of God keepeth himself, and that wicked one toucheth him not."**
>
> **1 John 5:18**

Even though God created your body to live forever, He did not create it to work ninety hours a week on little or no sleep and fueled by pizza, hamburgers, and French fries. You must respect the body God has given you. *"Know ye not that your body is the temple of the Holy Spirit,"* (1 Corinthians 3:16). The temple was a sacred place. Many Old Testament stories show how quickly the wrath of God fell upon those who defiled the temple and its holy artifacts.

This devotional is not about guilt, but motivation. Years ago, I made some notes for one of my leaders who had a tendency to be very critical of her voluntary staff. Despite my best efforts to teach her how to motivate her team, she still seemed obsessed with pointing out their shortcomings rather than setting the mark. I jotted this down to help her see the difference between a criticism and a challenge.

CRITICISM	vs.	CHALLENGE
Focus is on the future.		Focus is on the past.
Focus is on the minimum requirements.		Focus is on the maximum potential.
A criticism will wound.		A challenge will inspire.
Seeks to punish.		Seeks to improve.
Expresses disappointment.		Expresses confidence.
Constrains		Releases
Demoralizes		Empowers
Religious		Christ-like

Don't be critical of yourself; challenge yourself.

One thing I have often noticed with teenagers is that any kind of standard or restraint placed on them by their parents is viewed as a prison wall. It's not easy to convince a teenager that what they see as "prison walls" are really the walls of a fortress. They are not there to keep them trapped inside, but rather they are there to the keep all the bad trapped outside. When our forefathers settled the east coast and slowly began to move west, the first thing they did was build a fort. The Bible is full of stories about walled cities. It makes sense to try to create a perimeter of protection against any possible enemy attack.

The standard we raise concerning what we allow into our bodies is not about constraint, but protection. Each of us needs to build walls of moderation which hold at bay the dangerous health risks of obesity, diabetes, high blood pressure, and chronic infections, as well as a host of other potential health risks. As a believer who carries the precious Gospel of Jesus Christ, we have better things to do than to spend our time in a doctor's waiting room reading last year's magazines.

If an ounce of prevention is worth a pound of cure then we should use wisdom in our own personal health. Take a lesson from the great Apostle Paul. He was a man who was carried up into the third heaven and saw things not lawful for a man to utter. He wrote two-thirds of the New Testament and was so highly anointed that it is said when his hand-kerchief was placed on the sick, they recovered. When a man like that makes the statement, "I count not myself to have apprehended, but this one thing I do," you would do well to pay very close attention to what he is about to say.

> *"Brethren, I count not myself to have apprehended: but this one thing I do, forgetting those things which are behind, and reaching forth unto those things which are before, I press toward the mark for the prize of the high calling of God in Christ Jesus."*
>
> **Philippians 3:13-14**

Day 19

Leave the past in the past. Set new goals for your future. Don't settle for the low call; press toward the high call of God in Christ Jesus. Start where you are today and build a strong defense against sickness and disease. Don't let the devil steal another moment of your life! Do only what you can do and God will do what only He can do.

Scripture Meditations

"The God of my rock; in him will I trust: he is my shield, and the horn of my salvation, my high tower, and my refuge, my saviour; thou savest me from violence."

2 Samuel 22:3

"The LORD is my strength and my shield; my heart trusted in him, and I am helped: therefore my heart greatly rejoiceth; and with my song will I praise him."

Psalm 28:7

"Thou art my hiding place and my shield: I hope in thy word."

Psalm 119:114

"My goodness, and my fortress; my high tower, and my deliverer; my shield, and he in whom I trust; who subdueth my people under me."

Psalm 144:2

"No weapon that is formed against thee shall prosper; and every tongue that shall rise against

thee in judgment thou shalt condemn. This is the heritage of the servants of the LORD, and their righteousness is of me, saith the LORD."

Isaiah 54:17

"And put a knife to thy throat, if thou be a man given to appetite."

Proverbs 23:2

"We know that whosoever is born of God sinneth not; but he that is begotten of God keepeth himself, and that wicked one toucheth him not."

1 John 5:18

The Key to Heaven

"And the key of the house of David will I lay upon his
shoulder; so he shall open, and none shall shut;
and he shall shut, and none shall open."

Isaiah 22:22

eaven is a beautiful place with walls of jasper and
streets of gold. Also—and this should come as no
surprise—heaven is a place where there is no
sickness. What a comforting thought that believers can
look forward to a time of never having to worry about
the flu season or even cancer ever again. What is
exciting is the fact that Jesus has given us the keys to the
Kingdom of heaven and we can have access right now.

> **"And I will give unto thee the keys of the
> kingdom of heaven: and whatsoever thou
> shalt bind on earth shall be bound in heaven:
> and whatsoever thou shalt loose on earth
> shall be loosed in heaven."**
>
> **Matthew 16:19**

This is not only the power to access heaven, but
also the power to bind and to loose. To "bind" means
simply to "*forbid*" and to "loose" means to "*allow*."
We have the power to forbid and allow any thing

here on earth and have heaven back it up. These keys unlock the force of heaven. When you release something on earth, it is released in heaven. Heaven is the place where the Lord sits upon His throne and rules over the universe. This is where the messengers of God gather and report directly to the Lord as recorded in the book of Job. When you release something, the resources of heaven are unleashed to enforce that release.

Do you remember when Peter was in prison and the church came together for an all-night prayer vigil?[1] You really don't see very many of those anymore. This is an excellent example of how the church prayed for Peter's release and an angel was dispatched from heaven to let Peter out of prison. The prison doors swung open like a modern-day supermarket and the angel led Peter out. Peter headed over to the prayer meeting. I find it comical that when they came to the door, they thought Peter was a vision and didn't let him in at first.[2] Things can happen that will freak you out when you learn to bind and loose.

> When you release something, the resources of heaven are unleashed to enforce that release.

When Elisha was surrounded by the enemy, he told his servant, "Those who are with us are more than those who are against us."[3] This seemed a little strange to the servant since he could only see himself and the prophet starring down at a great host of *soldiers*. Elisha prayed, "Lord, open his eyes that he may see." Immediately, the servant perceived a host of angels in chariots of fire. These are the armies of heaven, ready to enforce what we forbid and allow.

In particular, the power to bind is so important when you have that feeling of being totally out of control. Have you ever felt the sensation of drowning? It's not a very pleasant feeling at all. You don't have to be swimming to feel it either. You can drown in a sea of bills or despair. But the power to bind allows us to tether ourselves in the spirit. The first thing a police officer will do when he makes an arrest is to handcuff the suspect. Well, we have the power to do the same thing to anything that comes against us. We have the authority to bind the devil in the Name of Jesus. You just have to remember that it is not our power, but the power of heaven working on our behalf.

"But we have this treasure in earthen vessels, that the excellency of the power may be of God, and not of us."

2 Corinthians 4:7

This power to bind and loose came at a great cost to our Lord and Savior. We should respect it and not try to use it to impose our will upon others. This can be a very subtle form of witchcraft. Binding and loosing were never meant to be a used for imposing our will on others, but rather as a means of experiencing God's will in our lives. Remember, what Jesus said as He taught His disciples to pray: *"Thy will be done on earth as it is in heaven,"* (Matthew 6:10). However, it's easy to pray in the will of the Lord, especially when we pray the Word. I am completely confident that it is the Lord's will to heal and you should not hesitate to bind sickness and loose healing into your situation. These aren't the keys to your carnal desires, but the keys to the Kingdom of heaven.

I am sure you've heard preachers talk about entering into the "promised land." This is in reference to the Lord bringing the Hebrews into the land of Canaan which had first been promised to Abraham. We enter into our "promised land" when we begin to unlock the promises of God's Word. The easiest way to know beyond all doubt that you are praying within the Lord's will is to find a promise in God's Word that speaks to your situation and use your Kingdom key to unlock it. Back in the day, we called it "standing on the promises of God."

There are some amazing events recorded in the Bible. If the Lord ever offered to take you back into time to visit one miraculous event in Scripture—and it could be only one—what would you choose? Moses parting the water? The walls of Jericho? Or, maybe even the resurrection of Lazarus would be awfully tempting. There is one event recorded in Luke that has to be close to the top of my list. That is, when the angels were singing to the shepherds announcing Jesus' birth.

> *"And suddenly there was with the angel a multitude of the heavenly host praising God, and saying, Glory to God in the highest, and on earth peace, good will toward men."*
>
> **Luke 2:13-14**

"Heavenly host" is a term that gets me excited. When Christ gave us the keys to the Kingdom of heaven it includes heaven's legions of angels. What incredible authority we have in the Name of Jesus. That Name is the key to power like we have never imagined. The angel of the Lord encamps round about them who believe (Psalm 34:7). They are not simply watching. When reading the stories of angels in the Scripture, they always had a mission. I don't ever remember reading about an angel who was on a break and just "came by" to chat with one of the Old Testament patriarchs. Angels do what they are assigned to do in military fashion. Christ has given us the rank and right to bind and loose, forbid and allow the mission of angels.

Jesus told His disciples in the very early days of His ministry that they would see the windows of heaven open and angels ascending and descending on the Son of Man (John 1:51). This was a reference to the miracles, signs, wonders, wisdom, and revelation that was about to be made manifest before their very eyes.

You see, Christ did not just *unlock* the door for us; He *gave* us the keys. Keys imply ownership. It is time to take a ride around the block in your spiritual authority.

Scripture Meditations

"And he lighted upon a certain place, and tarried there all night, because the sun was set; and he took of the stones of that place, and put them for his pillows, and lay down in that place to sleep. And he dreamed, and behold a ladder set up on the earth, and the top of it reached to heaven: and behold the angels of God ascending and descending on it."

Genesis 28:11-12

"Jesus answered and said unto him, Because I said unto thee, I saw thee under the fig tree, believest thou? thou shalt see greater things than these. And he saith unto him, Verily, verily, I say unto you, Hereafter ye shall see heaven open, and the angels of God ascending and descending upon the Son of man."

John 1:50-51

"And I say also unto thee, That thou art Peter, and upon this rock I will build my church; and the gates of hell shall not prevail against it. And I will give unto thee the keys of the kingdom of heaven: and whatsoever thou shalt bind on earth shall be bound in heaven: and whatsoever thou shalt loose on earth shall be loosed in heaven."

Matthew 16:18-19

"And he said unto them, When ye pray, say, Our Father which art in heaven, Hallowed be thy name. Thy kingdom come. Thy will be done, as in heaven, so in earth."

Luke 11:2

"And I heard a great voice out of heaven saying, Behold, the tabernacle of God is with men, and he will dwell with them, and they shall be his people, and God himself shall be with them, and be their God. And God shall wipe away all tears from their eyes; and there shall be no more death, neither sorrow, nor crying, neither shall there be any more pain: for the former things are passed away. And he that sat upon the throne said, Behold, I make all things new. And he said unto me, Write: for these words are true and faithful. And he said unto me, It is done. I am Alpha and Omega, the beginning and the end. I will give unto him that is athirst of the fountain of the water of life freely."

Revelation 21:3-6

Day 21

Hold On to Your Miracle

"Let us hold fast the profession of our faith without wavering; (for he is faithful that promised;)"

Hebrews 10:23

Jesus had a select group called His disciples that got the special HD/DVD version of His teachings. It had all the missing scenes and extra information that was not available to the general public. On one occasion, Christ tells the story of a sower who went forth to sow (Luke 8:4-15). Immediately, the fowls of the air came and consumed the seed before it could take root. The disciples got the inside story. The seed is the Word of God and the fowls of the air represent the devil. Satan comes and tries to the steal the Word of God before it can take root.

When the Lord heals your body, it is a manifestation of the Word of God in your life.

"He sent his word, and healed them, and delivered them from their destructions."

Psalm 107:20

Think about it like this. Each story about some-one being healed in the Bible actually became the Word of God. Look for yourself. Recorded in its pages is one story after another of someone receiving a miracle. When the Lord does a miracle in your life, it becomes a sermon; a living epistle to everyone around you. The book of Acts is the only book in the New Testament not to end with a benediction. That is because the *acts* of the Holy Spirit are *still* happening to this day. Every, single time the Holy Spirit moves, it's a fresh chapter to the unfolding story of the Spirit of God.

When your healing begins to take root, the devil will attempt to steal it. Theft is in the devil's Biblical job description.

"The thief cometh not, but for to steal, and to kill, and to destroy: . . ."

John 10:10

Don't let past disappointments and hurts keep you from trusting the Lord with all your heart.

The enemy comes before the seed can effectively take root and become permanent. This calls for two questions to be answered. First, how do we get this seed to take root? Secondly, how do we put a scarecrow in this garden to chase out the demonic crows? Getting the seed of the Word of God to take root in your life begins with the condition of the soil. You must be receptive to the seed. If the ground is hard, then the seed will just lie on top and become easy prey for the next hungry bird. A tender heart is the beginning of a lasting miracle. Don't let past disappointments and hurts keep you from trusting the Lord with all your heart.

As for the spiritual scarecrow, this is a good place for a cross. Trust in the miracle purchased for you at Calvary. Remind the devil of his utter defeat at Golgotha. (Golgotha means *"the place of the skull."*) I can promise you that just as soon as you begin to feel better, the devil is going to whisper in your ear that you are only imagining things. This battle takes place only in the mind. "This will never last"is the desperate cry of hell's black crows.

Satan is a serpent and can be very subtle. He will tell you things like, "Don't say anything to anyone until you are absolutely sure, that way you won't embarrass yourself."

> ***"And having spoiled principalities and powers, he made a shew of them openly, triumphing over them in it."***
>
> **Colossians 2:15**

This verse let's us know that if we are going to deal with the devil, we must do so openly. Rebuke the devil aloud. Tell anyone and everyone what the Lord has done for you. Don't be seduced into silence. Fire off the shotgun of faith and scare off those demonic crows.

> ***"And they overcame him by the blood of the Lamb, and by the word of their testimony; . . ."***
>
> **Revelation 12:11**

The last thing the devil is going to hang around for is someone who is praising the Lord for His promises.

Don't ever believe for even one second that God is going to take His miracle back.

The Bible says, *"So shall my word be that goeth forth out of my mouth: it shall not return unto me void, but it shall accomplish that which I please, and it shall prosper in the thing whereto I sent it,"* (Isaiah 55:11).

> **"Looking unto Jesus the author and finisher of our faith; . . ."**
>
> **Hebrews 12:2**

The message of a loving God to a lost world starts with this phrase, "In the beginning God," (Genesis 1:1). God is the Alpha—the first. Well, God is not just good at beginnings; He also is the Omega—the last. Our God is a great finisher. Whatever miracle He has begun in your life, He will complete it. Many miracles are lost because people settle for "improvement," rather than total victory.

Perhaps you haven't considered just how powerful your testimony will be when the Lord moves in your life. Imagine yourself free from pain both physical and emotional; you are whole from head to toe. Your family and co-workers are going to be the first to ask, "What happened?" instead of trying to force the Gospel into them like feeding a stubborn child: "Here comes the choo choo! Woo, woo!"

Miracles are the dinner bell of salvation. Because of their potential impact, the devil will not just sit quietly in the corner twiddling his horns while the Lord works a miracle in your life.

You might be wondering, *"When"*—if ever—*"is the devil going to let this thing alone?" "Does my miracle ever become so permanent that I will be left alone?"* There is a verse which gives me tremendous hope. The Bible says," *. . . for the devil is come down unto you, having great wrath, because he knoweth that he hath but a short time,"* (Revelation 12:12).

So, you're not going to have to fight the devil every day for the rest of your life for this miracle. You're just going to have to convince him that he is wasting his time on you. You see, the devil knows his time is running out. His sense of urgency will compel him to avoid wasting time on anyone who shows no signs of falling prey to his tricks.

I encourage you to take hold of your miracle and don't even blink for one second. Latch on like you do to a roller coaster safety bar and don't look back! It's time to take that hopeless feeling that used to plague you and give it back to the devil. Tell him, "Satan, if you are looking for easy prey, then you best look elsewhere!" Don't give up your miracle! Testify until it is so deep in you that nothing can uproot it.

You are saved.

You are delivered.

You are healed, in Jesus' Name.

Scripture Meditations

"Submit yourselves therefore to God. Resist the devil, and he will flee from you."

James 4:7

"Now the parable is this: The seed is the word of God. Those by the way side are they that hear; then cometh the devil, and taketh away the word out of their hearts, lest they should believe and be saved."

Luke 8:11-12

"Seeing then that we have a great high priest, that is passed into the heavens, Jesus the Son of God, let us hold fast our profession."

Hebrew 4:14

"But let him ask in faith, nothing wavering. For he that wavereth is like a wave of the sea driven with the wind and tossed. For let not that man think that he shall receive any thing of the Lord. A double minded man is unstable in all his ways."

James 1:6-8

"Above all, taking the shield of faith, wherewith ye shall be able to quench all the fiery darts of the wicked."

Ephesians 6:16

"(As it is written, I have made thee a father of many nations,) before him whom he believed, even God, who quickeneth the dead, and calleth those things which be not as though they were. Who against hope believed in hope, that he might become the father of many nations, according to that which was spoken, So shall thy seed be. And being not weak in faith, he considered not his own body now dead, when he was about an hundred years old, neither yet the deadness of Sara's womb: He staggered not at the promise of God through unbelief; but was strong in faith, giving glory to God; And being fully persuaded that, what he had promised, he was able also to perform."

Romans 4:17-21

Conclusion

"Now faith is the substance of things hoped for
the evidence of things not seen."

Hebrew 11:1

Faith is the evidence of that yet unseen promise of God. In faith, you can already see it, and it is by the faith that you will have it. Your miracle is already on the way.

Guard those things the Holy Spirit has revealed to you over these past three weeks. Value your faith above anything else in this world. This is not an end but a beginning. Today's faith is the foundation upon which the Lord will build your future and success. It is from faith to faith and glory to glory that we all travel forth into the presence of the Lord.

In this present age of moral decay, America has become for the first time in her history a post-Christian nation. It is our responsibility to walk in the blessing and favor of the Lord. Your testimony is needed. Your miracle is not just the manifestation of God's love and care for you, but for a lost and dying world as well. It is your Christian duty to believe God's Word and receive its full benefits.

We must continue to daily build up our faith.

"But you, dear friends, build yourselves up in your most holy faith and pray in the Holy Spirit."

Jude 1:20

Please don't ever underestimate the potential of your faith. It would seem to be Satan's greatest goal to undermine and destroy every believer's faith. Despite the accolades and accomplishments of "the great" Apostle Paul, as he faces Nero's chop block, his last words are not about the many epistle's he wrote or the many churches he planted or even the mighty miracles he performed.

"For I am now ready to be offered, and the time of my departure is at hand. I have fought a good fight, I have finished my course, I have kept the faith: Henceforth there is laid up for me a crown of righteousness, which the Lord, the righteous judge, shall give me at that day: and not to me only, but unto all them also that love his appearing."

2 Timothy 4:6

This is the real battle that is fought by every single believer—the fight to keep the faith.

Together, we have journeyed through many of the questions, trials, and fears which keep us from receiving everything the Lord has for us. It is my sincere desire that something has helped you to reach out and believe that "all things are possible with God"!

Notes

INTRODUCTION

[1] Gibson, Mel (Producer and Director). (2004). *The Passion of the Christ.* [Motion Picture]. United States: Icon Productions.

DAY 1: Does God Still Heal Today?

[1] Kantor, Mattis. (1993). *The Jewish Time Line Encyclopedia.* Lanham, MD: Jason Aronson, Incorporated.

DAY 2: Communion

[1] See John 6:35 and John 6:48.
[2] Transubstantiation is a Roman Catholic view of the eucharist (the elements of communion used to represent the body and the blood of Jesus Christ) actually became the literal body and blood of Jesus when taken. The bread became His body; the wine became His blood. Transignification simply means the elements of communion are used to signify and represent the body and blood of Jesus when taken.

DAY 3: John G. Lake

[1] Lindsay, Gordon. (1997). *John G. Lake - Apostle to Africa.* Dallas, TX: Christ for the Nations, Inc.
[2] ibid.
[3] ibid.
[4] ibid.
[5] ibid.

DAY 4: Why am I Sick?

[1] Strong, Dr. James. (1890, original). *Strong's Exhaustive Concordance of the Bible.* WORDsearch Corp. (Greek, #37).

[2] Substance. (2008). In *Merriam-Webster Online Dictionary*. Retrieved June 24, 2008, from http://www.merriam-webster.com/dictionary/ substance.

[3] See John 8:36.

[4] *The Praise and Worship Song Book - Revised Edition*. (TN: Brentwood-Benson). Song Title: We Have Come Into This House. Words and Music: Ballinger, Bruce. (1976). Sound III/Tempo Music Publications.

DAY 5: The Fear Factor

[1] http://www.thephobiaguide.com.

[2] http://www.eqhelp.com/Stress_Proof.htm.

DAY 7: Spirits of Affliction

[1] *Webster's Dictionary*.

[2] http://www.en.wikipedia.org/wiki/Ying_Yang

DAY 8: Fervent Prayer

[1] See Matthew 10:46-52.

[2] Strong, Dr. James. (1890, original). *Strong's Exhaustive Concordance of the Bible*. WORDsearch Corp. (Greek "energeo", #1754 from Greek 1756 (energes); to *be active, efficient:*-do, (be) effectual (fervent), be mighty in, shew forth self, work (effectually in).

DAY 10: Healing Forgiveness

[1] http://www.cwr.org.uk/.

[2] See Luke 23:34.

[3] Smedes, Lewis B. (1984). *Forgive and Forget: Healing the Hurts We Don't Deserve*. New York, NY: Harper Collins Publishers.

DAY 11: Prescription Music

[1] Words from the ABC television series, *The Love Boat,* theme song.

[2] See 2 Chronicles 20:15-29.

DAY 12: A Merry Heart

[1] Strong, Dr. James. (1890, original). *Strong's Exhaustive Concordance of the Bible.* WORDsearch Corp. (Greek, #3107).
[2] See Matthew 5:3-11.
[3] Commemoration of Martin Luther, Teacher, Reformer, 1546; http:// www.worldofquotes.com /author/Martin-Luther/1/ index. html.
[4] http://en.wikipedia.org/wiki/Amazing_Grace. "Amazing Grace" is a well-known Christian hymn. The words were written late in 1772 by Englishman John Newton. They first appeared in print in Newton's Olney Hymns (1779), which he worked on with William Cowper.

DAY 13: Smith Wigglesworth

[1] Lairdon, Roberts (compiled by). (2006) *Smith Wigglesworth on Prayer, Power and Miracles.* Shippensburg, PA: Destiny Image.
[2] Wigglesworth, Smith. Pentecostal Classics/Ever Increasing Faith by Smith Wigglesworth/Gospel Publishing House http:// www.mindofchrist.net/ 0001/index.htm. This link claims it is public domain.

DAY 15: Help Thou My Unbelief

[1] Agronomy. (2008). In *Merriam-Webster Online Dictionary.* Retrieved June 24, 2008, from http://www.merriam-webster.com /dictionary/ agronomy.

DAY 16: Take Action

[1] See 2 Kings 5:1-14.
[2] See Mark 7:33 and John 9:6.
[3] *Webster's Dictionary.*

DAY 17: Healing in the Old Testament

[1] Blank, Wayne. (2001). "How Many In The Exodus?" *The Church of God Daily Bible Study - A Ministry of God's Word.* http://www.keyway.ca/ htm2001/20010121.htm.
[2] See Acts 10:10-16.

DAY 20: The Key to Heaven

[1] See Acts 12:5-7.
[2] See Acts 12:13-15.
[3] See 2 Kings 6:16.

About the Author

James A. McFadden is the Senior Pastor of Trinity Life Center located in Shepherdsville, Kentucky where he has served for over seventeen years. He is an ordained minister with the Assemblies of God.

He served under his father, Pastor T. L. McFadden, at Family Worship Center in Painesville, Ohio as an associate minister for four years.

He is been married to Brenda, his wife of 21 years. They have three children and live in Louisville, Kentucky.

To order additional copies of

Are You Ready for a Miracle?
A 21-Day Healing Devotional

Or, to contact James McFadden, write to:

James McFadden Ministries
P.O. Box 295
Shepherdsville, KY 40165

502.543.3265 voice
502.543.3191 fax

Visit us online:

www.needtlc.org

For prayer, please call the 24-Hour
TLC Prayer Line:

1.866.NEEDTLC

Available for world-wide distribution.

For bookstore orders, please contact

Blaze Publishing House

P.O. Box 184

Mansfield, TX 76063

U.S.A.

817.473.9704 voice

817.886.3618 fax

www.blazepublishinghouse.com